BLISTER JONES

JOHN TAINTOR FOOTE

1st WORLD
LIBRARY
Literary Society

Blister Jones

John Taintor Foote

© 1st World Library, 2006
PO Box 2211
Fairfield, IA 52556
www.1stworldlibrary.com
First Edition

LCCN: 2006935241

Softcover ISBN: 1-4218-2494-9
Hardcover ISBN: 1-4218-2394-2
eBook ISBN: 1-4218-2594-5

Purchase *"Blister Jones"*
as a traditional bound book at:
www.1stWorldLibrary.com/purchase.asp?ISBN=1-4218-2494-9

1st World Library Literary Society

Giving Back to the World

"If you want to work on the core problem, it's early school literacy."

- James Barksdale, former CEO of Netscape

"No skill is more crucial to the future of a child, or to a democratic and prosperous society, than literacy."

- Los Angeles Times

Literacy... means far more than learning how to read and write... The aim is to transmit... knowledge and promote social participation."

- UNESCO

"Literacy is not a luxury, it is a right and a responsibility. If our world is to meet the challenges of the twenty-first century we must harness the energy and creativity of all our citizens."

- President Bill Clinton

"Parents should be encouraged to read to their children, and teachers should be equipped with all available techniques for teaching literacy, so the varying needs and capacities of individual kids can be taken into account."

- Hugh Mackay

I dedicate this, my first book, with awe and the deepest affection, to Mulvaney -Mowgil - Kim, and all the wonderful rest of them.

J. T. F.

A certain magazine, that shall be nameless, I read every month. Not because its pale contents, largely furnished by worthy ladies, contain many red corpuscles, but because as a child I saw its numbers lying upon the table in the "library," as much a part of that table as the big vase lamp that glowed above it.

My father and mother read the magazine with much enjoyment, for, doubtless, when its editor was young, the precious prose and poetry of Araminta Perkins and her ilk satisfied him not at all.

Therefore, in memory of days that will never come again, I read this old favorite; sometimes - I must confess it - with pain.

It chanced that a story about horses - aye, race horses - was approved and sanctified by the august editor.

This story, when I found it sandwiched between *Jane Somebody's Impressions Upon Seeing an Italian Hedge*, and three verses entitled *Resurgam*, or something like that, I straightway bore to "Blister" Jones, horse-trainer by profession and gentleman by instinct.

"What that guy don't know about a hoss would fill a book," was his comment after I had read him the story.

I rather agreed with this opinion and so - here is the book.

THE THOROUGHBRED

Lead him away! - his day is done,
His satin coat and velvet eye
Are dimmed as moonlight in the sun
Is lost upon the sky.

Lead him away! - his rival stands
A calf of shiny gold;
His masters kneel with lifted hands
To this base thing and bold.

Lead him away! - far down the past,
Where sentiment has fled;
But, gentlemen, just at the last,
Drink deep! - *the thoroughbred*!

CONTENTS

BLISTER

How my old-young friend "Blister" Jones acquired his remarkable nickname, I learned one cloudless morning late in June.

Our chairs were tipped against number 84 in the curving line of box-stalls at Latonia. Down the sweep of whitewashed stalls the upper doors were yawning wide, and from many of these openings, velvet black in the sunlight, sleek snaky heads protruded.

My head rested in the center of the lower door of 84. From time to time a warm moist breath, accompanied by a gigantic sigh, would play against the back of my neck; or my hat would be pushed a bit farther over my eyes by a wrinkling muzzle - for Tambourine, gazing out into the green of the center-field, felt a vague longing and wished to tell me about it.

The track, a broad tawny ribbon with a lace-work edging of white fence, was before us; the "upper-turn" with its striped five-eighths pole, not fifty feet away. Some men came and set up the starting device at this red and white pole, and I asked Blister to explain to me just what it meant.

"Goin' to school two-year-olds at the barrier," he explained. And presently - mincing, sidling, making futile leaps to get away, the boys on their backs standing clear above them in the short stirrups - a band of deer-like young thoroughbreds assembled, thirty feet or so from the barrier.

Then there was trouble. Those sweet young things performed, with the rapidity of thought, every lawless act known to the equine brain. They reared. They plunged. They bucked. They spun. They surged together. They scattered like startled quail. I heard squeals, and saw vicious shiny hoofs lash out in every direction; and the dust spun a yellow haze over it all.

"Those jockeys will be killed!" I gasped.

"Jockeys!" exclaimed Blister contemptuously. "Them ain't jockeys - they're exercise-boys. Do you think a jock would school a two-year-old?"

A man, who Blister said was a trainer, stood on the fence and acted as starter. Language came from this person in volcanic blasts, and the seething mass, where infant education was brewing, boiled and boiled again.

"That bay filly's a nice-lookin' trick, Four Eyes!" said Blister, pointing out a two-year-old standing somewhat apart from the rest. "She's by Hamilton 'n' her dam's Alberta, by Seminole."

The bay filly, I soon observed, had more than beauty - she was so obviously the outcome of a splendid and selected ancestry. Even her manners were aristocratic. She faced the barrier with quiet dignity and took no part in the whirling riot except to move disdainfully aside when it threatened to engulf her. I turned to Blister and found him gazing at the filly with a far-away look in his eyes.

"Ole Alberta was a grand mare," he said presently. "I see her get away last in the Crescent City Derby 'n' be ten len'ths back at the quarter. But she come from nowhere, collared ole Stonebrook in the stretch, looked him in the eye the last eighth 'n' outgamed him at the wire. She has a hundred 'n' thirty pounds up at that.

"Ole Alberta dies when she has this filly," he went on after a pause. "Judge Dillon, over near Lexington, owned her, 'n' Mrs.

Dillon brings the filly up on the bottle. See how nice that filly stands? Handled every day since she was foaled, 'n' never had a cross word. Sugar every mawnin' from Mrs. Dillon. That's way to learn a colt somethin'."

At last the colts were formed into a disorderly line.

"Now, boys, you've got a chance - come on with 'em!" bellowed the starter. "Not too fast . . ." he cautioned. "Awl-r-r-right . . . let 'em go-o-!"

They were off like rockets as the barrier shot up, and the bay filly flashed into the lead. Her slender legs seemed to bear her as though on the breast of the wind. She did not run - she floated - yet the gap between herself and her struggling schoolmates grew ever wider.

"Oh, you Alberta!" breathed Blister. Then his tone changed. "Most of these wise Ikes talk about the sire of a colt, but I'll take a good dam all the time for mine!"

Standing on my chair, I watched the colts finish their run, the filly well in front.

"She's a wonder!" I exclaimed, resuming my seat.

"She acts like she'll deliver the goods," Blister conceded. "She's got a lot of step, but it takes more'n that to make a race hoss. We'll know about *her* when she goes the route, carryin' weight against class."

The colts were now being led to their quarters by stable-boys. When the boy leading the winner passed, he threw us a triumphant smile.

"I guess she's bad!" he opined.

"Some baby," Blister admitted. Then with disgust: "They've hung a fierce name on her though."

"Ain't it the truth!" agreed the boy.

"What *is* her name?" I asked, when the pair had gone by.

"They call her Trez Jolly," said Blister. "Now, ain't that a hell of a name? I like a name you can kind-a warble." He had pronounced the French phrase exactly as it is written, with an effort at the "J" following the sibilant.

"Tres Jolie - it's French," I explained, and gave him the meaning and proper pronunciation.

"Traysyolee!" he repeated after me. "Say, I'm a rube right. Tra-aysyole-e in the stretch byano-o-se!" he intoned with gusto. "You can warble that!" he exclaimed.

"I don't think much of Blister - for beauty," I said. "Of course, that isn't your real name."

"No; I had another once," he replied evasively. "But I never hears it much. The old woman calls me 'thatdambrat,' 'n' the old man the same, only more so. I gets Blister handed to me by the bunch one winter at the New Awlin' meetin'."

"How?" I inquired.

"Wait till I get the makin's 'n' I'll tell you," he said, as he got up and entered a stall.

"One winter I'm swipin' fur Jameson," he began, when he returned with tobacco and papers. "We ships to New Awlins early that fall. We have twelve dogs - half of 'em hop-heads 'n' the other half dinks.

"In them days I ain't much bigger 'n a peanut, but I sure thinks I'm a clever guy. I figger they ain't a gazabo on the track can hand it to me.

"One mawnin' there's a bunch of us ginnies settin' on the

fence at the wire, watchin' the work-outs. Some trainers 'n' owners is standin' on the track rag-chewin'.

"A bird owned by Cal Davis is finishin' a mile-'n'-a-quarter, under wraps, in scan'lous fast time. Cal is standin' at the finish with his clock in his hand lookin' real contented. All of a sudden the bird makes a stagger, goes to his knees 'n' chucks the boy over his head. His swipe runs out 'n' grabs the bird 'n' leads him in a-limpin'.

"Say! That bird's right-front tendon is bowed like a barrel stave!

"This Cal Davis is a big owner. He's got all kinds of kale - 'n' he don't fool with dinks. He gives one look at the bowed tendon.

"'Anybody that'll lead this hoss off the track, gets him 'n' a month's feed,' he says.

"Before you could spit I has that bird by the head. His swipe ain't goin' to let go of him, but Cal says: 'Turn him loose, boy!' 'N' I'm on my way with the bird.

"That's the first one I ever owns. Jameson loans me a stall fur him. That night a ginnie comes over from Cal's barn with two bags of oats in a wheelbarrow.

"A newspaper guy finds out about the deal, 'n' writes it up so everybody is hep to me playin' owner. One day I see the starter point me out to Colonel King, who's the main squeeze in the judge's stand, 'n' they both laugh.

"I've got all winter before we has to ship, 'n' believe me I sweat some over this bird. I done everythin' to that tendon, except make a new one. In a month I has it in such shape he don't limp, 'n' I begins to stick mile gallops 'n' short breezers into him. He has to wear a stiff bandage on the dinky leg, 'n' I puts one on the left-fore, too - it looks better.

"It ain't so long till I has this bird cherry ripe. He'll take a-holt awful strong right at the end of a stiff mile. One day I turns him loose, fur three-eighths, 'n' he runs it so fast he makes me dizzy.

"I know he's good, but I wants to know *how* good, before I pays entrance on him. I don't want the clockers to get wise to him, neither!

"Joe Nickel's the star jock that year. I've seen many a good boy on a hoss, but I think Joe's the best judge of pace I ever see. One day he's comin' from the weighin'-room, still in his silks. His valet's with him carryin' the saddle. I steps up 'n' says:

"'Kin I see you private a minute, Joe?'

"'Sure thing, kid,' he says. 'N' the valet skidoos.

"'Joe,' I says, 'I've got a bird that's right. I don't know just how good he is, but he's awful good. I want to get wise to him before I crowds my dough on to the 'Sociation. Will you give him a work?'

"It takes an awful nerve to ask a jock like Nickel to work a hoss out, but he's the only one can judge pace good enough to put me wise, 'n' I'm desperate.

"'It's that Davis cripple, ain't it?' he asks.

"'That's him,' I says.

"He studies a minute, lookin' steady at me.

"'I'm your huckleberry,' he says at last. 'When do you want me?'

"'Just as she gets light to-morrow mawnin',' I says quick, fur I hasn't believed he'd come through, 'n' I wants to stick the gaff into him 'fore he changes his mind.

"He give a sigh. I knowed he was no early riser.

"'All right,' he says. 'Where'll you be?'

"'At the half-mile post,' I says. 'I'll have him warmed up fur you.'

"'All right,' he says again - 'n' that night I don't sleep none.

"When it begins to get a little gray next mawnin' I takes the bird out 'n' gallops him a slow mile with a stiff breezer at the end. But durin' the night I gives up thinkin' Joe'll be there, 'n' I nearly falls off when I comes past the half-mile post, 'n' he's standin' by the fence in a classy overcoat 'n' kid gloves.

"He takes off his overcoat, 'n' comes up when I gets down,'n' gives a look at the saddle.

"'I can't ride nothin' on that thing,' he says. 'Slip over to the jocks' room 'n' get mine. It's on number three peg - here's the key.'

"It's gettin' light fast 'n' I'm afraid of the clockers.

"'The sharp-shooters'll be out in a minute,' I says.

"'I can't help it,' says Joe. 'I wouldn't ride a bull on that saddle!'

"I see there's no use to argue, so I beats it across the center-field, cops the saddle 'n' comes back. I run all the way, but it's gettin' awful light.

"'Send him a mile in forty-five 'n' see what he's got left,' I says, as I throws Joe up.

"'Right in the notch - if he's got the step,' he says.

"I click Jameson's clock on them, as they went away - Joe

whisperin' in the bird's ear. The back-stretch was the stretch, startin' from the half. I seen the bird's mouth wide open as they come home, 'n' Joe has double wraps on him. 'He won't beat fifty under that pull!' I says to myself. But when I stops the clock at the finish it was at forty-four-'n'-three-quarters. Joe ain't got a clock to go by neither - that's judgin' pace! - take it from me!

"'He's diseased with speed,' says Joe, when he gets down. 'He can do thirty-eight sure - just look at my hands!'

"I does a dance a-bowin' to the bird, 'n' Joe stands there laughin' at me, squeezin' the blood back into his mitts.

"We leads the hoss to the gate, 'n' there's a booky's clocker named Izzy Goldberg.

"'You an exercise-boy now?' he asks Joe.

"'Not yet,' says Joe. 'Mu cousin here owns this trick, 'n' I'm givin' him a work.'

"'Up kind-a early, ain't you? Say! He's good, ain't he, Joe?' says Izzy; 'n' looks at the bird close.

"'Naw, he's a mutt,' says Joe.

"'What's he doin' with his mouth open at the end of that mile?' Izzy says, 'n' laughs.

"'He only runs it in fifty,' says Joe, careless. 'I takes hold of him 'cause he's bad in front, 'n' he's likely to do a flop when he gets tired. So long, Bud!' Joe says to me, 'n' I takes the bird to the barn.

"I'm not thinkin' Izzy ain't wise. It's a cinch Joe don't stall him. Every booky would hear about that work-out by noon. Sure enough the *Item's* pink sheet has this among the tips the next day:

John Taintor Foote

"'Count Noble' - that was the bird's name - 'a mile in forty-four. Pulled to a walk at the end. Bet the works on him; his first time out, boys!'

"That was on a Saturday. On Monday I enters the bird among a bunch of dogs to start in a five furlong sprint Thursday. I'm savin' every soomarkee I gets my hands on 'n' I pays the entrance to the secretary like it's a mere bag of shells. Joe Nickel can't ride fur me - he's under contract. I meets him the day before my race.

"'You're levelin' with your hoss, ain't you?' he says. 'I'll send my valet in with you, 'n' after you get yours on, he'll bet two hundred fur me.'

"'Nothin' doin', Joe!' I says. 'Stay away from it. I'll tell you when I gets ready to level. You can't bet them bookies nothin' - they're wise to him.'

"'Look-a-here, Bud!' says Joe. 'That bird'll cake-walk among them crabs. No jock can make him lose, 'n' not get ruled off.'

"'Leave that to me,' I says.

"Just as I figgers - my hoss opens up eight-to-five in the books.

"I gives him all the water he'll drink afore he goes to the post, 'n' I has bandages on every leg. The paddock judge looks at them bandages, but he knows the bird's a cripple, 'n' he don't feel 'em.

"'Them's to hold his legs on, ain't they?' he says, 'n' grins.

"'Surest thing you know,' I says. But I feels some easier when he's on his way - *there's seven pounds of lead in each of them bandages.*

"I don't want the bird whipped when he ain't got a chance.

"'This hoss backs up if you use the bat on him,' I says to the jock, as he's tyin' his reins.

"'He backs up anyway, I guess,' he says, as the parade starts.

"The bird gets away good, but I'd overdone the lead in his socks. He finished a nasty last - thirty len'ths back.

"'Roll over, kid!' says the jock, when I go up to slip him his fee. 'Not fur ridin' that hippo. It 'ud be buglary - he couldn't beat a piano!'

"I meets Colonel King comin' out of the judge's stand that evenin'.

"'An owner's life has its trials and tribulations - eh, my boy?' he says.

"'Yes, sir!' I says. That's the first time Colonel King ever speaks to me, 'n' I swells up like a toad. 'I'm gettin' to be all the gravy 'round here,' I says to myself.

"Two days after this they puts an overnight mile run fur maidens on the card, 'n' I slips the bird into it. I knowed it was takin' a chance so soon after his bad race, but it looks so soft I can't stay 'way from it. I goes to Cal Davis, 'n' tells him to put a bet down.

"'Oh, ho!' he says. 'Lendin' me a helpin' hand, are you?' Then I tells him about Nickel.

"'Did Joe Nickel work him out for you?' he says. 'The best is good enough fur you, ain't it? I'll see Joe, 'n' if it looks good to him I'll take a shot at it. Much obliged to you.'

"'Don't never mention it,' I says.

"'How do you mean that?' he says, grinnin'.

John Taintor Foote

"'Both ways,' says I.

"The mawnin' of the race, I'm givin' the bird's bad leg a steamin', when a black swipe named Duckfoot Johnson tells me I'm wanted on the phone over to the secretary's office, 'n' I gets Duckfoot to go on steamin' the leg while I'm gone.

"It's a feed man on the phone, wantin' to know when he gets sixteen bucks I owe him.

"'The bird'll bring home your coin at four o'clock this afternoon,' I tells him.

"'Well, that's lucky,' he says. 'I thought it was throwed to the birds, 'n' I didn't figure they'd bring it home again.'

"When I gets back there's a crap game goin' on in front of the stall, 'n' Duckfoot's shootin'. There's a hot towel on the bird's leg, 'n' it's been there too long. I takes it off 'n' feel where small blisters has begun to raise under the hair - a little more 'n' it 'ud been clear to the bone. I cusses Duckfoot good, 'n' rubs vaseline into the leg."

I interrupted Blister long enough to inquire:

"Don't they blister horses sometimes to cure them of lameness?"

"Sure," he replied. "But a hoss don't work none fur quite a spell afterwards. A blister, to do any good, fixes him so he can't hardly raise his leg fur two weeks.

"Well," he went on, "the race fur maidens was the last thing on the card. I'm in the betting-ring when they chalks up the first odds, 'n' my hoss opens at twenty-five-to-one. The two entrance moneys have about cleaned me. I'm only twenty green men strong. I peels off ten of 'em 'n' shoved up to a booky.

"'On the nose fur that one,' I says, pointin' to the bird's name.

"'Quit your kiddin',' he says. 'What 'ud you do with all that money? This fur yours.' 'N' he rubs to twelve-to-one.

"'Ain't you the liberal gink?' I says, as he hands me the ticket.

"'I starts fur the next book, but say! - the odds is just meltin' away. Joe's 'n' Cal's dough is comin' down the line, 'n' the gazabos, thinkin' it's wise money, trails. By post-time the bird's a one-to-three shot.

"I've give the mount to Sweeney, 'n' like a nut I puts him hep to the bird, 'n' he tells his valet to bet a hundred fur him. The bird has on socks again, but this time they're empty, 'n' the race was a joke. He breaks fifth at the get-away, but he just mows them dogs down. Sweeney keeps thinkin' about that hundred, I guess, 'cause he rode the bird all the way, 'n' finished a million len'ths in front.

"I cashes my ticket, 'n' starts fur the barn to sleep with that bird, when here comes Joe Nickel.

"'He run a nice race,' he says, grinnin', 'n' hands me six hundred bucks.

"What's this fur?' I says. 'You better be careful . . . I got a weak heart.'

"'I win twelve hundred to the race,' he says. "N' we splits it two ways.'

"'Nothin' doin',' I says, 'n' tries to hand him back the wad.

"'Go awn!' he says, 'I'll give you a soak in the ear. I bet that money fur you, kiddo.'

"I looks at the roll 'n' gets wobbly in the knees. I never see so much kale before - not at one time. Just then we hears the announcer sing out through a megaphone:

"'The o-o-owner of Count Nobul-l-l-l is wanted in the judge's stand!'

"'Oy, oy!' says Joe. 'You'll need that kale - you're goin' to lose your happy home. It's Katy bar the door fur yours, Bud!'

"'Don't worry - watch me tell it to 'em,' I says to Joe, as I stuffs the roll 'n' starts fur the stand. I was feelin' purty good.

"'Wait a minute,' says Joe, runnin' after me. 'You can't tell them people nothin'. You ain't wise to that bunch yet. Bud - why, they'll kid you silly before they hand it to you, 'n' then change the subject to somethin' interestin', like where to get pompono cooked to suit 'em. I've been up against it,' he says, "'n' I'm tellin' you right. Just keep stallin' around when you get in the stand, 'n' act like you don't know the war's over.'

"'Furget it,' I says. 'I'll show those big stiffs where to head in. I'll hypnotize the old owls. I'll give 'em a song 'n' dance that's right!'

"As I goes up the steps I see the judges settin' in their chairs, 'n' I takes off my hat. Colonel King ain't settin', he's standin' up with his hands in his pockets. Somehow, when I sees *him* I begins to wilt - he looks so clean. He's got a white mustache, 'n' his face is kind-a brown 'n' pink. He looks at me a minute out of them blue eyes of his.

"'Are you the owner of Count Noble, Mr. - er - ?'

"'Jones, sir,' I says.

"'Jones?' says the colonel.

"'Yes, sir,' I says.

"'Mr. Jones,' says the colonel, 'how do you account for the fact that on Thursday Count Noble performs disgracefully, and on Saturday runs like a stake horse? Have the days of the week anything to do with it?'

"I never says nothin'. I just stands there lookin' at him, foolin' with my hat.

"'This is hell,' I thinks.

"'The judges are interested in this phenomenon, Mr. Jones, and we have sent for you, thinking perhaps you can throw a little light on the matter,' says the colonel, 'n' waits fur me again.

"'Come on . . . get busy!' I says to myself. 'You can kid along with a bunch of bums, 'n' it sounds good - don't get cold feet the first time some class opens his bazoo at you!' But I can't make a noise like a word, on a bet.

"'The judges, upon looking over the betting sheets of the two races in which your horse appeared, find them quite interesting,' says the colonel. 'The odds were short in the race he did *not* win; they remained unchanged - in fact, rose - since only a small amount was wagered on his chances. On the other hand, these facts are reversed in to-day's race, which he *won*. It seems possible that you and your friends who were pessimists on Thursday became optimists today, and benefited by the change. Have you done so?'

"I see I has to get some sort-a language out of me.

"'He was a better hoss to-day - that's all I knows about it,' I says.

"'The *first* part of your statement seems well within the facts,' says the colonel. 'He was, apparently, a much better horse to-day. But these gentlemen and myself, having the welfare of the American thoroughbred at heart, would be glad to learn by what method he was so greatly improved.'

John Taintor Foote

"I don't know why I ever does it, but it comes to me how Duckfoot leaves the towel on the bird's leg, 'n' I don't stop to think.

"'I blistered him,' I says.

"'You - *what?*' says the colonel. I'd have give up the roll quick, sooner'n spit it out again, but I'm up against it.

"'I blisters him', I says.

"The colonel's face gets red. His eyes bung out 'n' he turns 'round 'n' starts to cough 'n' make noises. The rest of them judges does the same. They holds on to each other 'n' does it. I know they're givin' me the laugh fur that fierce break I makes.

"'You're outclassed, kid!' I says to myself. 'They'll tie a can to you, sure. The gate fur yours!'

"Just then Colonel King turns round, 'n' I see I can't look at him no more. I looks at my hat, waitin' fur him to say I'm ruled off. I've got a lump in my throat, 'n' I think it's a bunch of bright conversation stuck there. But just then a chunk of water rolls out of my eye, 'n' hits my hat - pow! It looks bigger'n Lake Erie, 'n' 'fore I kin jerk the hat away - pow! - comes another one. I knows the colonel sees 'em, 'n' I hopes I croak.

"'Ahem -', he says.

"'Now I get mine!' I says to myself.

"'Mr. Jones,' says the colonel, 'n' his voice is kind-a cheerful. 'The judges will accept your explanation. You may go if you wish.'"

Just as I'm goin' down the steps the colonel stops me.

"'I have a piece of advice for you, Mr. Jones,' he says. His voice ain't cheerful neither. It goes right into my gizzard. I turns and looks at him. '*Keep that horse blistered from now on!*' says the colonel.

"Some ginnies is in the weighin'-room under the stand, 'n' hears it all. That's how I gets my name."

TWO RINGERS

"Hello, ole Four Eyes!" was the semi-affectionate greeting of Blister Jones. "I ain't seed you lately."

I had found him in the blacksmith shop at Latonia, lazily observing the smith's efforts to unite Fan Tan and a set of new-made, blue-black racing-plates. I explained how a city editor had bowed my shoulders with the labors of Hercules during the last week, and began to acquire knowledge of the uncertainties connected with shoeing a young thoroughbred.

A colored stable-boy stood at Fan Tan's wicked-looking head and addressed in varied tone and temper a pair of flattened ears.

"Whoa! Baby-doll! Dat's ma honey - dat's ma petty chile - . . . Whoa! Yuh no-'coun' houn', yuh!" The first of the speech had been delivered soothingly, as the smith succeeded in getting a reluctant hind leg into his lap; the last was snorted out as the leg straightened suddenly and catapulted him into a corner of the shop, where he sat down heavily among some discarded horseshoes.

The smith arose, sweat and curses dripping from him.

"Chris!" said Blister, "it's a shame the way you treat that pore filly. She comes into yer dirty joint like a little lady, fur to get a new pair of shoes, 'n' you grabs her by the leg 'n' then cusses her when she won't stand fur it."

Part of the curses were now directed at Blister.

"Come on, Four Eyes," he said. "This ain't no place fur a minister's son."

"I'd like to stay and see the shoeing!" I protested, as he rose to go.

"What shoeing?" he asked incredulously. "You ain't meanin' a big strong guy like Chris manhandlin' a pore little filly? Come awn - I can't stand to see him abusin' her no more."

We wandered down to the big brown oval, and Blister, perching himself on the top rail of the fence, took out his stopwatch, although there were no horses on the track.

"What are you going to do with that?" I asked.

"Got to do it," he grinned. "If I was to set on a track fence without ma clock in my mitt, I'd get so nur-r-vous! Purty soon I'd be as fidgity as that filly back there. Feelin' this ole click-click kind-a soothes my fevered brow."

In a silence that followed I watched a whipped-cream cloud adrift on the deepest of deep blue skies.

"Hi, hum!" said Blister presently, and extending his arms in a pretense of stretching, he shoved me off the fence. "You're welcome," he said to my protests, and added: "There's a nice matched pair."

A boy, leading a horse, was emerging from the mouth of a stall.

The contrast between them was startling - never had I seen a horse with so much elegant apparel; rarely had I seen a boy with so little. The boy, followed by the horse, began to walk a slow circle not far from where we sat. Suddenly the boy addressed Blister.

John Taintor Foote

"Say, loan me the makin's, will you, pal?" he drawled.

From his hip pocket Blister produced some tobacco in a stained muslin bag and a wad of crumpled cigarette papers. These he tossed toward the boy.

"Yours trooly," muttered that worthy, as he picked up the "makin's". "Heard the news about Hicky Rogers?" he asked, while he rolled a cigarette.

"Nothin', except he's a crooked little snipe," Blister answered.

"Huh! that ain't news," said the boy. "They've ruled him off - that's what I mean."

"That don't surprise me none," Blister stated. "He's been gettin' too smart around here fur quite a while. It'll be a good riddance."

"Were you ever ruled off the track?" I asked Blister, as the boy, exhaling clouds of cigarette smoke, returned to the slow walking of his horse. He studied in silence a moment.

"Yep - once," he replied. "I got mine at New Awlins fur ringin' a hoss. That little ole town has got my goat."

"When was this?" I asked.'

"The year I first starts conditionin' hosses," he answered.

I had noticed that dates totally eluded Blister. A past occurrence as far as its relation to time was concerned, he always established by a contemporary event of the turf. Pressed as to when a thing had taken place he would say, "The year Salvation cops all the colt stakes," or "The fall Whisk-broom wins the Brooklyn Handicap." This had interested me and I now tried to get something more definite from him. He answered my questions vaguely.

"Say, if you're lookin' fur that kind of info," he said at last, "get the almanac or the byciclopedia. These year things slide by so easy I don't get a good pike at one, 'fore another is not more'n a len'th back, 'n' comin' fast."

I saw it was useless.

"Well, never mind just when it happened," I said. "Tell me about it."

"All right," said Blister. "Like I've just said it happens one winter at New Awlins, the year after I starts conditionin' hosses.

"Things break bad fur me that winter. Whenever a piker can't win a bet he comes 'round, slaps me on the wrist, 'n' separates me from some of my kale. I'm so easy I squeezes my roll if I meets a child on the street. The cops had ought to patrol me, 'cause larceny'll sure be committed every time a live guy speaks to me.

"I've only got three dogs in my string. One of 'em's a mornin'-glory. He'll bust away as if he's out to make Salvator look like a truck-hoss, but he'll lay down 'n' holler fur some one to come 'n' carry him when he hits the stretch. One's a hop-head 'n' I has to shoot enough dope into him to make him think he's Napoleon Bonyparte 'fore he'll switch a fly off hisself. Then when he sees how far away the wire is he thinks about the battle of Waterloo 'n' says, 'Take me to Elby.'

"I've got one purty fair sort of a hoss. He's just about ready to spill the beans, fur some odds-on, when he gets cast in the stall 'n' throws his stifle out. The vet. gets his stifle back in place.

"'This hoss must have a year's complete rest,' he says.

"'Yes, Doc,' I says. "N' when he gets so he can stand it, how'd a trip to Europe do fur him?'

"Things go along like this till I'm busted right. No, I ain't busted - I'm past that. I owes the woman where I eats, I owes the feed man, I owes the plater, 'n' I owes every gink that'll stand fur a touch.

"One day a messenger boy comes 'n' leans against the stall door 'n' pokes a yellow envelope at me.

"'Well, Pierpont,' I says, 'what's the good word?'

"'Sign here. Two bits,' he says, yawnin'.

"I sees where it says 'charges paid,' 'n' I takes him by the back of the neck 'n' he gets away to a flyin' start fur the gate. The message is from Buck Harms.

"'Am at the St Charles, meet me nine a. m. to-morrow,' it says.

"This Harms duck is named right, 'cause that's what he does to every guy he meets. He's so crooked he can sleep on a corkscrew. When there ain't nobody else around he'll take money out of one pocket 'n' put it in another. He's been ruled off twict 'n' there's no chance fur him to get back. I wouldn't stand fur him only I'm in so bad I has to do somethin'.

"'If he takes any coin from me he'll have to be Hermann,' I says to myself, 'n' I shows up at the hotel the next mawnin'.

"Harms is settin' in the lobby readin' the dope-sheet. I pipes him off 'n' he don't look good to me fur a minute, but I goes over 'n' shakes his mitt.

"'Well, Blister, old scout, how're they breakin'?' he says.

"'So, so,' I says.

"'That right?' he says. 'I hears different. Fishhead Peters tells me they've got you on the ropes.'

"'What th' hell does that gassy Fishhead know about me?' I says.

"'Cut out the stallin',' he says. 'It don't go between friends. Would you like to git a-holt of a new roll?'

"'I don't mind tellin' you that sooner 'n have my clothes tore I lets somebody crowd a bundle of kale on to me,' I says.

"'That sounds better,' he says. 'Come on - we'll take a cab ride.'

"'Where we goin'?' I asks him, as we gets into a cab.

"'Goin' to look at a hoss,' he says.

"'What fur?' I says.

"'Wait till we git there 'n' I'll tell you,' he says.

"We rides fur about a hour 'n' pulls up at a barn out in the edge of town. We goes inside 'n' there's a big sorrel geldin', with a blaize face, in a box-stall.

"'Look him over,' says Harms. I gets one pike at the hoss -

"'Why! it's ole Friendless!' I says.

"'Look close,' he says. 'Wait till I get him outside.'

"I looks the hoss over careful when he's outside in the light, 'n' I don't know what to think. First I think it's Friendless 'n' then I think maybe it ain't.

"'If it ain't Friendless, it's his double!' I says at last. 'But I think Friendless has a white forefoot.'

"'Well, it ain't Friendless,' says Harms as he leads the hoss into the barn. 'And you're right about the white foot.'

"Now, Friendless is a bird that ain't started fur a year. Harms or some of his gang used to own him, 'n' *believe me*, he can *ramble some* if everythin' 's done to suit him. He's a funny hoss, 'n' has notions. If a jock'll set still 'n' not make a move on him, Friendless runs a grand race. But if a boy takes holt of him or hits him with the bat, ole Friendless says, 'Nothin' doin' to-day!' 'n' sulks all the way. He'd have made a great stake hoss only he's dead wise to how much weight he's packin'. He'll romp with anythin' up to a hundred 'n' ten, but not a pound over that can you slip him. Looks like he says to hisself, 'They must think I'm a movin' van,' 'n' he lays his ole ears back, 'n' dynamite won't make him finish better'n fourth. This little habit of his'n spoils him 'cause he's too good, 'n' the best he gets from a handicapper is a hundred 'n' eighteen - that kind of weight lets him out.

"Goin' back in the cab Harms tells me why he sends fur me. This dog he's just showed me 's named Alcyfras. He's been runnin' out on the coast 'n' he's a mutt - he can't beat a fat man. Harms sees him one day at Oakland, 'n' has a guy buy him.

"Harms brings this pup back East. He has his papers 'n' description all regular. The guy that buys him ain't wise - he's just a boob Harms is stallin' with. What he wants me to do is to take the hoss in my string, get him identified 'n' start him a couple of times; then when the odds is real juicy I'm to start Friendless under the dog's name 'n' Harms 'n' his gang'll bet him to a whisper at the poolrooms in Chicago 'n' New York.

"'Where's Friendless now?' I asks him.

"'They're gettin' him ready on a bull-ring up in Illinois,' says Harms. 'He's in good shape 'n' 'll be dead ripe time we get ready to ship him down here. I figure we'll put this gag across about Christmas.'

"'What does the boy wonder get fur swappin' mules with the Association?' I says. 'I'm just dyin' to know what Santa Claus'll bring little Alfred.'

"'You get all expenses, twenty-five bucks a week, 'n' a nice slice of the velvet when we cleans up,' says Harms.

"'Nix, on that noise!' says I. 'If you or some other benevolent gink don't crowd five hundred iron dollars on G. Percival the day before the bird flies, he won't leave the perch.'

"'Don't you trust me?' says Harms.

"'Sure,' I says, 'better'n Cassie Chadwick.'

"He argues, but it don't get him nothin' so he says he'll come across the day before Friendless brings home the bacon, 'n' I make him cough enough to pay what I owes. The next day a swipe leads Alcyfras out to the track.

"'What's the name of that dog?' Peewee Simpson yells, as I'm cross-tyin' the hoss at the stall door.

"'Alcyfras,' I says, as I pulls the blanket off. Peewee comes over 'n' looks at the hoss a minute.

"'Alcy nothin'!' he says. 'If that ain't Friendless, I never sees him.'

"I digs up the roll Harms give me.

"I'll gamble this pinch of spinach his name is Alcyfras,' I says.

"'You kin name what you like far as I'm concerned, 'n' change it every mawnin' before breakfast,' says Peewee. 'But if you starts him as anythin' but Friendless we don't see your freckled face 'round here no more.'

"By this time a bunch has gathered 'n' soon there's a swell argument on. One guy'll say it's Friendless 'n' another 'll say it ain't. Finally somebody says to send fur Duckfoot Johnson, who swiped Friendless fur two years. They send for him.

"When Duckfoot comes he busts through the crowd like he's the paddock judge.

"'Lemme look at dis hoss,' he says.

"Everybody draws back 'n' Duckfoot looks the hoss over 'n' then runs his hand under his barrel close to the front legs.

"'No, sah, dis ain' Frien'less,' he says. 'Frien'less has a white foot on de off front laig and besides dat he has a rough-feeling scab on de belly whar he done rip hisself somehow befo' I gits him. Dis dawg am smooth as a possum.'

"That settles all arguments. You can't fool a swipe 'bout a hoss he's taken care of. He knows every hair on him.

"One day I'm clockin' this Alcyfras while a exercise-boy sends him seven-eights. When I looks at my clock I thinks they ought to lay a thousand-to-one against the mutt, after he starts a couple of times. Just then somethin' comes 'n' stands in front of me 'n' begins to make little squeaky noises.

"'Are you Mr. Blister?' it says.

"I bats my eyes 'n' nods.

"'I've got 'em again,' I thinks.

"'Oh, what a relief!' it squeaks. 'I just thought I'd never find you. I've been looking all over the race course for you!'

"'Gracious! Ferdy, you've had a awful time, ain't you?' I says. 'If you want to stay out of trouble, read your *Ladies' Home Journal* more careful.'

"'My name is Alcibides Tuttle,' says pink toes, drawin' hisself up. 'And I am the owner of the horse called Alcyfras. I purchased this animal upon the advice of my friend, Mr. Harms, whom I met in San Francisco.'

"Say! I've worked fur some nutty owners, but this yap's the limit.

"'Well, Alci, here comes Alcy now,' I says, as the boy comes up with the dog, 'n' my new boss stretches his number three neck out of his number nine collar 'n' blinks at the hoss.

"Alcibides comes back to the stall with me 'n' from then on he sticks to me tighter 'n a woodtick. He's out to the track every mawnin' by nine 'n' he don't leave till after the races. He asks me eighty-seven squeaky questions a minute all the time we're together. I calls him 'n' his hoss both Alcy fur a while, but I changes him to Elsy - that was less confusin' 'n' it suits him better.

"The next week I starts Alcyfras among a bunch of crabs in a seven furlong sellin' race, 'n' the judges hold up his entrance till I can identify him. I hands them his papers 'n' they looks up the description of Friendless in the stud-book, where it shows he's got one white foot. Then they wire to the breeder of Alcyfras 'n' to the tracks in California where the dog has started. The answers come back all proper 'n' to cinch it I produce Elsy as owner. They look Elsy over while he tells 'em he's bought the hoss.

"'Gentlemen,' says Colonel King to the other judges, 'the mere sight of Mr. Tuttle has inspired me with full confidence in his entry and himself.' He bows to Elsy 'n' Elsy bows to him. The rest of the judges turn 'round 'n' look at somethin' over across the center-field.

"I tells Elsy his hoss is all to the merry, but we don't want him to win till the odds get right. He's standin' beside me at the race, 'n' Alcyfras runs next to last.

"'Of course, I realize you are more familiar with horse racing

John Taintor Foote

than myself,' he says; 'but I think you should have allowed him to do a little better. What method did you employ to make him remain so far in the rear?'

"'I tells the jock to pull him,' I says. The boy was usin' the bat half the trip, but Elsy never tumbles.

"'What do you say to a jockey when you desire him to lose?' Elsy asks me.

"'I just say - "Grab this one,"' I says.

"'What do you say when you require him to win?' he squeaks.

"'I don't say nothin'. I hands him a ticket on the hoss 'n' the jock wins if he has to get down 'n' carry the dog home,' I says.

"Not long after this, Friendless gets in from Illinois. I look him over in the car 'n' I see he's not ready. He's not near ready.

"'What kind of shoemakers give this hoss his prep.?' I asks Harms.

"'What's wrong with him?' he says. 'He looks good to me.'

"'He ain't ready,' I says. 'Look at him 'n' feel him! He'll need ten days more work 'n' a race under his belt 'fore he's safe to bet real money on.'

"Harms buys some stuff at a drug store, 'n' gets busy with the white fore-foot.

"'Only God A'mighty can make as good a sorrel as that!' he says when he's through. 'Here's the can of dope. Don't let her fade.'

"'What are you goin' to do about this Elsy person?' I says. 'While I ain't sayin' it's pure joy to have him around, I ain't got the heart to hand it to him. I don't mind trimmin' boobs -

that's what they're for - but this Elsy thing is too soft. He must be in quite a wad on this bum hoss of his'n.'

"'Who's Elsy?' says Harms.

"I tells him, 'n' he laughs.

"'Is that what you call him?' he says. 'What's bitin' you - ain't Friendless goin' to win a nice purse for him?'

"About ten o'clock that night Alcyfras goes out one gate 'n' Friendless comes in another. I keeps the foot stained good, 'n' shuts the stall door whenever Duckfoot shows up. In ten days the hoss is right on edge 'n' one race'll put the finish on him, so I enter him, in a bunch of skates, as Alcyfras. I gives the mount to Lou Smith - he ain't much of a jock, but he'll ride to orders. Just before the race I has a heart to heart talk with Lou.

"'Fur this hoss to win you don't make a move on him,' I says. 'If you hand him the bat or take hold of him at the get-away he sulks.'

"'All right, I lets him alone,' says Lou.

"'When I'm ready fur you to let him alone I slips you a nice ticket on this bird. You ain't got a ticket to-day, have you?' I says.

"'Not so's you could notice,' says Lou.

"'Are you hep?' I says.

"'I got-cha, Bo,' says Lou.

"I see Lou's arm rise 'n' fall a couple of times at the start 'n' ole Friendless finished fifth, his ears laid back, sulkier 'n a grass widow at a married men's picnic.

"'You let him do better to-day,' says Elsy. 'Isn't it time to allow

John Taintor Foote

him to win?'

"'He wins his next out,' I says.

"I tell Harms we're ready fur the big show 'n' I looks fur a nice race to drop the good thing into. But it starts to rain 'n' it keeps it up a week. Friendless ain't a mudder 'n' we has to have a fast track fur our little act of separating the green stuff from the poolrooms. I'm afraid the bird stales off if I don't get a race into him, so I enters him among a pretty fair bunch of platers, to keep him on edge.

"Three days before the race the weather gets good 'n' the track begins to dry out fast. I see it's goin' to be right fur my race 'n' I meets Harms 'n' tells him to wire his bunch to bet their heads off.

"'I don't like this race,' he says, when he looks at the entries. 'There's two or three live ones in here. This Black-jack ain't such a bad pup, 'n' this here Pandora runs a bang-up race her last out. Let's wait fur somethin' easier.'

"'Well, if you ain't a sure-thing better, I never gets my lamps on one!' I says. 'Don't you want me to saw the legs off the rest of them dogs to earn my five hundred? You must have forgot ole Friendless. He's only got ninety-six pounds up! He'll tin can sure! He kin fall down 'n' roll home faster than them kind of hosses.'

"But Harms won't take a chance, so I goes back to the track 'n' I was sore.

"'That guy's a hot sport, not!' I thinks.

"I hates to tell Elsy the hoss he thinks is his won't win - he'd set his little heart on it so. I don't tell him till the day before the race, 'n' he gets right sassy about it. I never see him so spunky.

"'As owner, I insist that you allow Alcyfras to win this race,' he says, 'n' goes away in a pet when I tells him nix.

"The day of the race I don't see Elsy at all.

"'You ain't got a ticket to-day, 'n' you know the answer,' I says to Lou Smith as the parade starts. He don't say nothin' but nods, so I think he's fixed.

"When I come through the bettin' ring I can't believe my eyes. There's Alcyfras at four-to-one all down the line. He opened at fifty, so somebody has bet their clothes on him.

"'Where does all this play on Alcyfras come from?' I says to a booky.

"'A lost shrimp wanders in here and starts it,' says the booky.

"'What does he look like?' I says.

"'Like a maiden's prayer,' says the booky, 'n' I beats it out to the stand.

"Elsy is at the top of the steps lookin' kind of haughty, 'n' say! - he's got a bundle of tickets a foot thick in his hand.

"'What dead one's name is on all them soovenirs?' I says, pointin' to the tickets.

"'Mr. Blister,' he says, 'after our conversation yesterday I made inquiry concerning the rights of a trainer. I was informed that a trainer, as a paid employee, is under the direction of the owner - his employer. You refused to allow my horse to win, contrary to my wishes. You had no right to do so. I intend that he *shall* win, and have wagered accordingly - these tickets are on Alcyfras.' He's nervous 'n' fidgity, 'n' his voice is squeakier 'n ever.

"'Well, Mr. Belmont,' I says, 'did you happen to give

John Taintor Foote

instructions to any more of your employees, your jockey, fur instance?'

"'I have adopted the method you informed me was the correct one,' he says, swellin' up. 'I gave a ticket at fifty-to-one calling for one hundred and two dollars to Mr. Smith, and explained to him that I was the owner.'

"Before Elsy gets through I'm dopey. I looks over his tickets 'n' he figures to win eight thousand to the race. I have two iron men in my jeans - I don't even go down 'n' bet it.

"'What's the use?' I says to myself.

"I can't hardly see the race, I'm so groggy from the jolt Elsy hands me. Friendless breaks in front and stays there all the way. Lou Smith just sets still 'n' lets the hoss rate hisself. That ole hound comes down the stretch a-rompin', his ears flick-flackin' 'n' a smile on his face. He wins by five len'ths 'n' busts the track record fur the distance a quarter of a second.

"Then it begins to get brisk around there. I figger to have Alcyfras all warmed up outside the fence the day Friendless wins. After the race I'd put *him* in the stall 'n' send Friendless out the gate. Elsy, practisin' the owner act, has gummed the game - Alcyfras is over in the other end of town.

"Ole Friendless bustin' the track record is the final blow. I don't hardly get to the stall 'fore here comes the paddock judge 'n' his assistant.

"'We want this hoss and you, too, over at the paddock,' he says. 'What's the owner's name?'

"'Alcibides Tuttle,' I says.

"'Is that all?' says the paddock judge. 'Go get him, Billy!' he says to his assistant. 'You'll likely find him cashin' tickets.'

"When we gets to the paddock, there's Colonel King and the rest of the judges.

"'Take his blanket off,' says the colonel, when we leads in the hoss.

"'He's red-hot, Colonel,' I says.

"'So am I,' says the colonel. 'Who was caretaker for the horse Friendless when he was racing?' he asks some of the ginnies.

"'Duckfoot Johnson,' says the whole bunch at once.

"'Send for him,' says the colonel.

"'I's hyar, boss,' says Duckfoot, from the back of the crowd.

"'Come and look this horse over,' says the colonel.

"'I done looked him over befo', boss,' says Duckfoot, when he gets to the colonel.

"'When?' says the colonel. 'When did you see him?'

"''Bout a month ago,' says Duckfoot.

"'Did you recognize him?' says the colonel.

"'Yes, sah,' says Duckfoot, 'I done recnomize him thoully fum his haid to his tail, but I ain' never seed him befo'.'

"'Recnomize him again,' the colonel tells him.

"'Boss,' says Duckfoot, 'some folks 'low dis hoss am Frien'less, but hit ain'. Ef hits Frien'less, an' yo' puts yo' han' hyar on his belly dey is a rough-feelin' scab. Dis hoss am puffeckly smo-o - ' then he stops 'n' begins to get ashy 'round the mouth.

"'Well?' says the colonel. 'What's the matter?'

John Taintor Foote

"'Lawd Gawd, boss! *Dis am Frien'less . . . Hyar's de scah*!' says Duckfoot, his eyes a-rollin'. Then he goes 'round 'n' looks at the hoss in front. 'Whar his white foot at?' he asks the colonel.

"'That's what we are about to ascertain,' says the colonel. 'Boy,' he says to a ginny, 'run out to the drug store with this dollar and bring me back a pint of benzine and a tooth-brush.'

"The ginny beats it.

"'You may blanket this horse now,' the colonel says to me.

"When the ginny gets back, Colonel King pours the benzine on the tooth-brush 'n' goes to work on the off-forefoot. It ain't long till it's nice 'n' white again.

"'That is most remarkable!' says Elsy, who's watchin' the colonel.

"'In my opinion, Mr. Tuttle,' says the colonel, 'the only remarkable feature of this affair is yourself. I can't get you properly placed. The Association will take charge of this horse until the judges rule.'

"The next day the judges send fur me 'n' Elsy. It don't take Colonel King thirty seconds to rule me off - I don't get back fur two years, neither! Then the colonel looks at Elsy.

"'Mr. Tuttle,' he says, 'if your connection with this business is as innocent as it seems, you should be protected against a further appearance on the turf. On the other hand, if you have acted a part in this little drama, the turf should be protected against you. In either case the judges desire to bring your career as an owner to a close; and we hereby bar you and your entries from all tracks of the Association. This is final and irrevocable.'

"Three years after that I'm at Hot Springs, 'n' I drops into McGlade's place one night to watch 'em gamble. There's a slim guy dealin' faro fur the house, 'n' he's got a green eye-shade on. All of a sudden he looks up at me.

"'Blister,' he says, 'do you ever tumble there's two ringers in the New Awlins deal? Me 'n' Buck Harms has quite a time puttin' it over - without slippin' you five hundred.'

"It's Elsy! 'N' say! - *his voice ain't any squeakier 'n mine!*"

John Taintor Foote

WANTED - A RAINBOW

At our last meeting Blister had told me of a "ringing" in years gone by that had ended disastrously for him. And now as we idled in the big empty grand-stand a full hour before it would be electrified by the leaping phrase, "They're off!" I desired further reminiscences.

"Ringing a horse must be a risky business?" I ventured.

"Humph!" grunted Blister, evidently declining to comment on the obvious. Then he glanced at me with a dry whimsical smile. "I see that little ole pad stickin' out of your pocket," he said. "Ain't she full of race-hoss talk yet?"

"Always room for one more," I replied, frankly producing the note-book.

"Well, I guess I'm the goat," he said resignedly. "I *had* figured to sick you on to Peewee Simpson to-day, but he ain't around, so I'll spill some chatter about ringin' a hoss among the society bunch one time, 'n' then I'll buy a bucket of suds."

"*I'll* buy the beer," I stated with emphasis.

"All right - just so we get it - I'll be dryer'n a covered bridge," said Blister.

"This ringin' I mentions," he went on, "happens while I'm ruled off.

"At the get-away I've got a job with a Chicago buyer, who used to live in New York. This guy has a big ratty barn. He deals mostly in broken-down skates that he sells to pedlers 'n' cabmen. Once in a while he takes a flier in high-grade stuff, 'n' one day he buys a team of French coach hosses from a breedin' farm owned by a millionaire.

"Believe me they was a grand pair - seal brown, sixteen hands 'n' haired like babies. They fans their noses with their knees, when get's the word, 'n' after I sits behind 'em 'n' watches their hock-action fur a while I feels like apologizin' to 'em fur makin' 'em haul a bum like me.

"These dolls go East,' says the guy I works fur. 'They don't pull no pig-sticker in this burg. They'll be at the Garden so much they'll head fur Madison Square whenever they're taken out.'

"He ships the pair East 'n' sends me with 'em as caretaker. I deliver 'em to a swell sales company up-town in New York.

"This concern has some joint - take it from me - every floor is just bulgin' with hosses that's so classy they sends 'em to a manicure parlor 'stead of a blacksmith's shop.

"There's a big show-ring, with a balcony all 'round it, on the top floor. They take my pair up there 'n' hook 'em to a hot wagon painted yellow, 'n' the company's main squeeze, named Brown, comes up to see 'em act. I'm facin' the door just as a guy starts to lead a hoss into the show-ring. The pair swings by, this hoss shies back sudden 'n' I see him make a queer move with his off rear leg. Brown don't see it - he's got his back to the door.

"The guy leads the hoss up to us.

"'Here's that hunter I phoned you about, Mr. Brown,' he says. The hoss is a toppy trick - bright bay, short backed, good coupled 'n' 'll weigh eleven hundred strong. But he's got a knot on his near-fore that shows plain.

"'I thought you told me he was sound?' says Brown, lookin' at the knot.

"'What's the matter with you, Mr. Brown?' says the guy. 'That little thing don't bother him. Any eight-year-old hunter that knows the game is bound to be blemished in front.'

"'Can you tell an unsound one when you look at him?' Brown asks me.

"'I can smell a dink a mile off,' I says.

"'Here's an outside party,' says Brown; 'let's hear what he has to say. Feel that bump, young man!' he says to me.

"I runs my hand over the knot.

"'That don't hurt him,' I says. 'It's on the shin 'n' part of it's thick skin.'

"'There!' says the guy. 'Your own man's against you.'

"'He's not my man,' says Brown, lookin' at me disgusted.

"'This ain't my funeral,' I says to Brown. ''N' I ain't had a call to butt in. If you tells me to butt - I butts.'

"'Go to it,' says Brown.

"'Do you throw a crutch in with this one?' I says to the guy.

"'What does he need a crutch for?' he says, givin' me a sour look.

"I takes the hoss by the head, backs him real sudden, 'n' he lifts the off-rear high 'n' stiff.

"'He's a stringer,' I says.

"Brown gives the guy the laugh.

"'You might get thirty dollars from a Jew pedler for him,' he says. 'He'll make a high-class hunter - for paper, rags and old iron.'

"'How did you know that horse was string-halted so quick?' says Brown to me when the guy has gone.

"'I told you I can smell a dink,' I says. But I don't tell him what I sees at the door.

"'I think we could use you and your nose around here,' he says. 'Are you stuck on Chicago?'

"'Me fur this joint,' I says, lookin' 'round. 'Do I have to get my hair waved more 'n' twict a week?'

"'We'll waive that in your case,' he says, laughin' at his bum joke.

"'Don't do that again,' I says. 'I've a notion to quit right here.'

"'I'd hate to lose an old employee like you - I'll have to be more careful,' he says - 'n' I'm workin' fur Mr. Brown.

"About a week after this, I'm bringin' a hackney up to the showroom fur Brown to look at, when a young chap dressed like a shoffer stops me.

"'I wish to see Mr. Brown, my man,' he says. 'Can you tell me where he is?'

"No shofe can spring this 'my man' stuff on *me*, 'n' get away with it. But a blind kitten can see this guy's all the gravy. There's somethin' about him makes you think the best ain't near as good as he wants. I tells him to come along with me, 'n' when we gets up to the showroom he sticks a card at Brown.

"'Yes, indeed - Mr. Van Voast!' says Brown, when he squints at the card. 'You're almost the only member of your family I have been unable to serve. I believe I have read that you are devoted to the motor game.'

"'That's an indiscretion I hope to rectify - I want a hunter,' says the young chap.

"'Take that horse down and bring up Sally Waters,' says Brown to me.

"This Sally Waters is a chestnut mare that's kep' in a big stall where she gets the best light 'n' air in the buildin'. A lot of guys have looked at her, but the price is so fierce nobody takes her.

"'Is that the best you have?' says the young chap, when I gets back with her.

"'Yes, Mr. Van Voast,' says Brown. 'And she's as good as ever stood on four legs! She'll carry your weight nicely, too.'

"'Is she fast?' says the young chap.

"'After racing at ninety miles an hour, anything in horse-flesh would seem slow to you, I presume,' says Brown. 'But she is an extremely fast hunter, and very thorough at a fence.'

"'Do you know Ferguson's Macbeth?' says the young chap.

"'I ought to,' says Brown. 'We imported Macbeth and Mr. Ferguson bought him from me.'

"The young chap studies a minute.

"'I might as well tell you that I want a hunter to beat Macbeth for the Melford Cup,' he says at last.

"'Oh, oh!' says Brown. 'That's too large an order, Mr. Van Voast - I can't fill it.'

"'You don't think this mare can beat Macbeth?' says the young chap.

"'No, sir, I do not,' says Brown. 'Nor any other hunter I ever saw. There might be something in England that would be up to it, but I don't know what it would be - and money wouldn't buy it if I knew.'

"The young chap won't look at the mare no more, 'n' Brown tells me to put her up. I hustles her back to the stall, 'n' goes down to the street door 'n' waits. There's a big gray automobile at the curb, with six guns stickin' out of her side in front - she looks like a battle-ship. Pretty soon the young chap comes out 'n' starts to board her 'n' I braces him.

"'I think I know where you can get the hoss you're lookin' fur,' I says.

"He stares at me kind-a puzzled fur a minute.

"'Oh, yes, you are the man who brought the mare up-stairs,' he says. 'What leads you to believe you can find a hunter good enough to beat Macbeth?'

"'I ain't said nothin' about a hunter,' I says. 'Would you stand fur a ringer?'

"'I think I get your inference,' he says. 'Be a little more specific, please.'

"'If I puts you hep to a hoss that ain't no more a hunter than that automobile,' I says, 'but can run like the buzz-wagon 'n' jump like a hunter - could you use him in your business?'

John Taintor Foote

"'What sort of a horse would that be?' he says.

"'A thoroughbred,' I says. 'A bang-tail.'

"'Oh - a runner,' he says. 'Do you know anything about the runners?'

"'A few,' I says. 'I'm on the track nine years.'

"'What are you doing here?' he says.

"'Ruled off,' I says.

"'Hm-m!' he says. 'What for?'

"'Ringin',' I says.

"'You seem to run to that sort of thing,' he says. 'What's your name?' he asks.

"'Blister Jones,' I says.

"'Delightful!' he says. 'I'm glad I met you. Who has this remarkable horse?'

"'Peewee Simpson,' I says.

"'Equally delightful! I'd like to meet him, too,' he says.

"'He's in Loueyville,' I says.

"'Regrettable,' he says. 'What's the name of his horse?'

"'Rainbow,' I says.

"'And I thought this was to be a dull day,' he says. 'Jump in here and take a ride. I don't know that I care to go rainbow-chasing assisted by Blisters, and Peewees - but nefarious undertakings have always appealed to me, and I desire to cultivate your acquaintance.'

"We goes fur a long ride in the battle-ship. He don't say much - just asks questions 'n' listens to my guff. At last I opens up on the Rainbow deal, 'n' I tries all I know to get him goin' - I sure slips him some warm conversation.

"'You heard what Brown said of Macbeth!' he says. 'Why are you so certain this Rainbow can beat him in a steeplechase?'

"'Why, listen, man!' I says. 'This Rainbow is the best ever. He can beat any brush-topper now racin' if the handicapper don't overload him. *He's* been coppin' where they race your eyeballs off. *He's* been makin' good against the real thing. *He's a thoroughbred!* If *he* turns in one of these here parlor races fur gents, with a bunch of hunters, *they won't know which way he went!*'

"'The runners I have seen are all neck and legs. They don't look like hunters at all,' he says.

"'You're thinkin' about these here flat-shouldered sprinters,' I says. 'This Rainbow is a brush-topper. He's got a pair of shoulders on *him* 'n' he's the jumpin'est thoroughbred ever I saw. Course he's rangier 'n most huntin'-bred hosses, but with a curb to put some bow in his neck, he'll pass fur a hunter anywhere!'

"'There is one sad thing I haven't told you,' he says. 'I must ride the horse myself.'

"'What's sad about that?' I says. 'You ain't much over a hundred 'n' forty, at a guess.'

"'The trouble is not with my weight - it's my disposition,' he says. 'I have not ridden for ten years. In fact I never rode much. To tell you the truth - I'm afraid of a horse.'

"Say - I'd liked that young chap fine till then! I think he's

John Taintor Foote

handin' me a josh at first.

"'You're kiddin' me, ain't you?' I says.

"'No,' he says. 'I'm not kidding you. I've fought my fear of horses since I was old enough to think. Lately it has become necessary for me to ride, and I'm going to do it - it it kills me!'

"We were back to my joint by this time 'n' he looks at me 'n' laughs.

"'Cheer up!' he says. 'I'll think over what you told me and let you know. I go over to Philadelphia to-morrow to race in a "buzz-wagon," as you call it. I don't want you to think me entirely chicken-hearted - and I'll take you with me, if Brown can spare you.'

"The next day he shows up in the battle-ship.

"'Blister,' he says, 'I don't know just how far I'll be willing to go in the affair, but if you can get Rainbow, I'll buy him.'

"'Now you've said somethin',' I says. 'Head fur the nearest telegraph office 'n' I'll wire Peewee.'

"'They're likely to ask a stiff price fur this hoss,' I says when we gets to the telegraph office.

"'Buy him,' he says.

"'*Do you mean the sky's the limit?*' I says, 'n' he nods.

"We cross on the ferry after sendin' the wire. He has the battle-ship under wraps till we hit the open country, 'n' then he lets her step. We gets to goin' faster 'n' faster. I can't see, 'n' I think my eyebrows have blowed off. I'm so scared I feel like my stumick has crawled up in my chest, but I hopes this is the limit, 'n' I grits my teeth to keep from yelpin'. Just then we hits a long straight road, 'n' what we'd been doin' before seemed like backin' up. I can't breathe 'n' I can't stand no more of it.

"'Holy cats!' I yells. 'Cut it!'

"'What's the matter?' he says, when he's slowed down.

"'Holy cats!' I says again. 'Is that what racin' in these things is like?'

"'Oh, no,' he says. 'My mechanic took my racing car over yesterday. This is only a roadster.'

"'Only a - what?' I says.

"'Only a roadster - a pleasure car,' he says.

"'Oh - a pleasure car,' I says. 'It's lucky you told me.'

"'It's all in getting accustomed to it,' he says.

"I spends the night at a hotel in Philadelphia with a guy named Ben, who's the mechanic, 'n' the next mawnin' I sees the race. Say! Prize-fightin', or war, or any of them little games is like button-button to this automobile racin'! They kills two guys that day 'n' why they ain't all killed is by me. The young chap finishes second to some Eyetalian - but that Dago sure knowed he'd been in a race.

""'N' he's the guy that's afraid of a hoss!' I says to myself. 'Now, wouldn't that scald you?'

"When he leaves me at my joint in New York the young chap writes on a card 'n' hands it to me.

"'Here's my name and present address,' he says. 'Let me know when you hear from our friend Peewee.'

"Printed on the card is 'Mr. William Dumont Van Voast,' 'n'

John Taintor Foote

in pencil, 'Union Club, New York City.'

"The next day I gets a wire from Peewee in answer to mine.

"'Sound as a dollar. Eighteen hundred bones buys him. P. W. Simpson,' it says.

"I phones Mr. Van, 'n' he says to go to it - so I wires Peewee.

"'Check on delivery if sound. You know me. Ship with swipe first express. Blister Jones.'

"In two days Duckfoot Johnson leads ole Rainbow into the joint, 'n' I tells Brown it's a hoss fur Mr. Van. I looks him over good 'n' he's O. K. I gets Mr. Van on the phone 'n' he comes up 'n' writes a check fur eighteen hundred, payable to Peewee. He gives this to Duckfoot, slips him twenty-five bucks fur hisself, 'n' hands him the fare back to Loueyville besides.

"'What next?' says Mr. Van to me. 'Do we need a burglar's kit, and some nitroglycerin, or does that class of crime come later?'

"'We want a vet. right now,' I says. 'This bird has got to lose some tail feathers.'

"'Well, you are the chief buccaneer!' says Mr. Van. 'I'll serve as one of the pirate crew at present. When you have the good ship Rainbow shortened at the stem and ready to carry the jolly Roger over the high seas - I should say, fences - let me know. In the meantime,' he says, slippin' me five twenties, 'here are some pieces-of-eight with which to buy cutlasses, hand grenades and other things we may need.'

"I has the vet. dock Rainbow's tail, 'n' as soon as it heals I lets Mr. Van know. He tells me to bring the hoss to Morrisville, New Jersey, on the three o'clock train next day.

"When I unloads from the express car at Morrisville, there's Mr. Van and a shoffer in the battle-ship.

"'Just follow along behind, Blister!' says Mr. Van, 'n' drives off slow down the street.

"We go through town 'n' out to a big white house, with pillars down the front. Mr. Van stops the battle-ship at the gates.

"'Take the car to the Williamson place - Mr. Williamson understands,' he says to the shofe.

"I wonders why he stops out here - it's a quarter of a mile to the house. When we gets to the house there's an old gent, with gray hair, settin' on the porch. He gets up when he sees us, 'n' limps down the steps with a cane.

"'Don't disturb yourself, Governor!' says Mr. Van. 'Anybody here?'

"'No, I'm alone,' says the old gent. 'Your sister is with the Dandridges. Your man came this morning, so I was expecting you.' Then he looks at Rainbow. 'What's that?' he says.

"'A horse I've bought,' says Mr. Van. 'I'm thinking of going in for hunting.'

"'Oh! *She's* brought you to it, has she?' says the old gent. '*I* never could. Why do you bring the horse here?'

"Mr. Van flushes up.

"'You know what a duffer I am on a horse, Governor,' he says. 'Well, I want to try for the Melford Cup. I'd like to build a course on the place, and school myself under your direction.'

"'Ah, ha!' says the old gent. 'And then the conquering hero will descend on Melford, to capture the place in general, and one of its fair daughters in particular!'

"'Something like that,' says Mr. Van.

John Taintor Foote

"'I'll be glad to help you all I can,' says the old gent, 'just so long as you don't bring one of those stinking things you usually inhabit on these premises!'

"'It's a bargain. I've already sent the one I came in to Ralph Williamson,' says Mr. Van, 'n' we takes Rainbow to the stables.

"I liked Mr. Van's old man right away, 'n' when he finds out I knows as much about a hoss as he does, he treats me like a brother.

"He gets busy quick, 'n' has the men fix up a mile course on the place with eight fences in it - some of 'em fierce.

"'Twice around, and you have the Melford course to a dot,' he says. 'Now, young man,' he says to me, 'you get the horse ready and I'll go to work on the rider.' 'N' believe me, he does it.

"His bum leg won't let him ride no more, but he puts Mr. Van on a good steady jumper, 'n' drives besides the course in a cart, tellin' him what to do. He keeps Mr. Van goin' till I think he'll put him out of business - 'n' say! - but he cusses wicked when things don't go to suit him!

"'Stick your knees in and keep your backbone limber! Hold his head up now at this jump - *don't drag at his mouth that way*! Why! damn it all! . . . you haven't as good hands as a cab-driver,' is the kind of stuff he keeps yellin' at poor Mr. Van.

"I'm workin' Rainbow each day, 'n' in three weeks I take him twice around the course at a good clip.

"'The hoss'll do in another week,' I says to the old gent.

"'I'll be ready fur you,' he says, shuttin' his mouth, 'n' that was the worst week of all for Mr. Van. But he improved wonderful, 'n' one mawnin' he takes Rainbow over the course at speed.

"'Not half bad!' says the old gent when they come back. 'He's not up to his horse yet,' he says to me. 'But between 'em they'll worry that Melford crowd some, or I miss my guess!'

"A day or so after that we starts for Melford. The old gent says good-by to me, 'n' then he sticks out his mitt at Mr. Van.

"'God bless you, boy!' he says. 'I wish you luck both in the race and - elsewhere.'

"Say, this Melford is the horsiest burg ever I saw! They don't do nothin' but ride 'em 'n' drive 'em 'n' chew the rag about 'em - men 'n' women the same. Even the kids has toppy little ponies and has hoss shows fur their stuff.

"They has what they call a Hunt Club, 'n' everybody hangs out there. This club gives the cup Mr. Van wants to win. The race fur it is pulled off once a year, 'n' only club members can enter.

"The Ferguson guy has won the race twice with the Macbeth hoss 'n' if he wins it again he keeps the cup. The race is due in two weeks, but there ain't much talk about it - everybody knows Ferguson'll win sure.

"This Ferguson has all the kale in the world. He lives in a house so big it looks like the Waldorf. But from what I hear, the bloods ain't so awful strong fur him - except his ridin', they all take their hats off to that.

"There's a girl named Livingston 's the best rider among the dames, 'n', believe me, she's a swell doll - she's the niftiest filly I ever gets my lamps on - she's all to the peaches 'n' cream.

"It don't take me long to see that Mr. Van is nutty, right, about this one, but it looks like Ferguson has the bulge on him, 'cause her 'n' Ferguson is always out in front when they chase the hounds, 'n' they ride together a lot. We're at Mr. Van's brother's place, 'n' when we first get there Mr. Van puts

John Taintor Foote

me wise.

"'Blister,' he says, 'you must now assume the disguise of a groom. While you and I know we are partners in crime, custom requires an outward change in our heretofore delightful relationship - keep your eyes open and act accordingly.'

"I'm dead hep to what he means, 'n' when I'm rigged up like all the rest of the swipes around there, I touches my hat to him whenever he tells me anythin'.

"Everybody joshes Mr. Van about his ridin', but they get over that sudden - the first time he chases hounds with 'em ole Rainbow 'n' him stays right at the head of the procession. I'm waitin' at the club to take the hoss home after the run. When Mr. Van is turnin' him over to me Miss Livingston comes up.

"'I'm so *proud* of you!' she says to him. 'It was splendid . . . I told you you could do anything you tried!'

"'Rainbow's the chap who deserves your approval,' says Mr. Van, pointin' to the hoss.

"'Indeed, he does - the old precious!' she says, 'n' rubs her face against Rainbow's nose. Just then Ferguson rides up with a English gink who's a friend of Mr. Van's, 'n' the dame beats it into the club-house. This Englishman is a lord or a duke or somethin', 'n' he's visitin' Mr. Van's brother. Ferguson ain't on Macbeth. He's rode a bay mare that day, 'n' Rainbow has outrun 'n' out-jumped her.

"'That's quite a horse you have there, Van,' Ferguson says. 'A bit leggy - isn't he?'

"'Perhaps he is,' says Mr. Van. 'But I like something that can get over the country.'

"'Going to enter him for the cup?' says Ferguson.

"'I don't know yet,' says Mr. Van, careless. 'I must see the committee, and tell them his antecedents - this horse rather outclasses most hunters.'

"'He doesn't outclass mine, over the cup course, for five thousand!' says Ferguson, gettin' red.

"'Done!' says Mr. Van, quiet-like. 'If the committee says I'm eligible we'll settle it in the cup race. If not, we can run a match.'

"'Entirely satisfactory,' says Ferguson, 'n' starts to go. But he comes back, 'n' looks at Mr. Van wicked. 'By the way,' he says, 'money doesn't interest either of us at present. Suppose we raise the stake this way - the loser will take a trip abroad, for a year, and in the meantime we both agree to let matters rest - in a certain quarter.'

"'Done!' says Mr. Van again. He looks at the other guy colder 'n ice when he says it.

"Ferguson nods to him 'n' rides off.

"The English gink has heard the bet, 'n' when Ferguson beats it he shakes his head.

"'Aw, old chap!' he says. 'That's a bit raw - don't you think? I'm sorry you let him draw you. It's a beastly mess.'

"'I'm not afraid of him and his horse!' says Mr. Van. But I can see he ain't feelin' joyous.

"'Damn him and his hawss - and you too!' says the English gink. 'Aw, it's the young girl you've dragged into it, Billy!'

"'It's a confidential matter, and no names were mentioned,' says Mr. Van.

"'Don't quibble, old chap!' says the English gink. 'The name's nothing. And as for its being confidential - Ferguson is sure to tell that - aw - French puppy he's so thick with, and the viscawnt'll be - aw - tea-tabling it about by five o'clock!'

"'You're right, of course,' says Mr. Van, slow. 'It was a low thing to do - a cad's trick. No wonder you English are so rotten superior. You don't need brains - the right thing's bred into your bones. Your tempers never show you up. We revert to the gutter at the pinch.'

"'Oh, I say! That's bally nonsense!' says the English gink. 'I would have done the same thing.'

"'Not unless the fifteen hundred years it's taken to make you were wiped off the slate,' says Mr. Van. 'However, I'll have to see it through now.'

"The guys that run the club say Rainbow can start in the cup race. Mr. Van tells me, 'n' the next week I watch him while he sends the hoss over the course. We're comin' up towards the club-house, after the work-out, 'n' we run into Miss Livingston. She hands Mr. Van the icy stare 'n' he starts to say something but she breaks in.

"'I wonder you care to waste any words on a mere racing wager,' she says.

"'Please let me try to explain . . .' says Mr. Van.

"'There can be no explanation. What you did was the act of a boor - and a fool,' says the dame, 'n' walks on by.

"I think over what she says. 'She's more sore cause she thinks he'll lose than anythin' else,' I says to myself. 'He ain't in so bad, after all.' But Mr. Van don't tumble. He's awful glum from then on.

"There's a fierce mob of swells at the course the day of the race, classy rigs as far as you can see. The last thing I says to

Mr. Van is:

"'You've got the step of them any place in the route, but you're on a thoroughbred, 'n' he'll run hisself into the ground if you let him. You don't know how to rate him right - so stay close to the Macbeth hoss till you come to the last fence, then turn Rainbow loose, 'n' he'll make his stretch-run alone.'

"There's six entries, but the race is between Rainbow and Macbeth from the get-away. Macbeth is a black hoss, 'n' I never believed till then a hunter could romp that fast. He was three len'ths ahead of the field at the first fence, with Rainbow right at his necktie. They gets so far ahead, nobody sees the other starters from the second fence on. Mr. Van rides just like I tells him, 'n' lets the black hoss make the pace. Man! - that hunter did run! Towards the end both hosses begin to tire, but the clip was easier fur the thoroughbred, 'n' I see Rainbow's got the most left.

"Before they come to the last fence Mr. Van turns his hoss loose like I tells him, 'n' he starts to come away from Macbeth. My! but those swells did holler! They never thought Rainbow has a chance. At the last fence he's a len'th in front, 'n' right there it happens Mr. Van don't take hold of him enough to keep his head up, 'n' he blunders at the fence 'n' comes down hard on his knees. Mr. Van slides clear to the hoss's ears, 'n' the crowd gives a groan as Macbeth comes over 'n' goes by.

"'He's gone!' I says to myself, 'n' I can't believe it when he gets back in the saddle somehow 'n' starts to ride. But the black hoss has a good six len'ths 'n' now two hundred yards to go.

"'He'll never reach . . .' I says out loud. 'He'll never reach . . .'

"Then Rainbow begins his stretch-run with the blood comin' out of his knees, 'n' while he's a tired hoss, a gamer one never looks through a bridle. I ain't knockin' that hunter - there was no canary in him, but I think a game thoroughbred's the gamest hoss that lives!

John Taintor Foote

"Ole Rainbow is a straight line from his nose to his tail. His ears is flat 'n' his mouth's half open fur air. Every jump he takes looks thirty feet long 'n' he's gettin' to the black hoss fast. I'm watchin' the distance to go 'n' all of a sudden I furgets where I am -.

"'He wins sure as hell!' I hollers.

"'Oh, will he?' says a voice. I looks up 'n' there's Miss Livingston sittin' on her hoss, her fists doubled up 'n' her face whiter'n chalk.

"About ten len'ths from the finish Rainbow gets to the black 'n' they look each other in the eye. But them long jumps of the thoroughbred breaks the hunter's heart, 'n' Rainbow comes away, 'n' wins by a len'th. . . .

"After I've cooled Rainbow out, 'n' bandaged his knees at the club stables, I starts fur home with him.

"I'm just leavin' the main road, to take the short cut, when Miss Livingston gallops by, with a groom trailin'. She looks up the cross-road, sees me 'n' the hoss, 'n' reins in. She says somethin' to the groom 'n' he goes on.

"Miss Livingston comes up the crossroad alone, 'n' stops when she gets to us.

"'Is that Rainbow?' she says.

"'Yes'm,' I says.

"'Help me down, please,' she says. I tries to do it, but I don't make a good job of it.

"'You're not a lady's groom?' she says, smilin'.

"'No'm,' I says.

"'I should like to pat the winner;' she says. 'May I?'

"'Go as far as you like,' I says.

"'I beg pardon?' she says, lookin' at me funny.

"'Yes'm, you can pat him,' I says.

"She takes Rainbow by the head, 'n' sort of hugs it, 'n' rubs the tips of her fingers over his eyelids. Then she whispers to him, but I hears it.

"'Old precious!' she says. 'I've always loved Rainbows! Do you bring a fair day, too?'

"Just then a black auto sneaks around the bend of the main road, 'n' Mr. Van's drivin' it. He sees us, stops, 'n' comes up the side road to where we are. She don't hear him till he's right close. Then she backs away from Rainbow.

"'I thought you might become tired of your sudden interest in hunting, Mr. Van Voast,' she says. 'And I should like to own this horse - I was just looking at him,' she tries to say it haughty, but it don't seem to scare him none. He looks at her steady.

"'If I give you a rainbow, will you give me its equivalent?' he says.

"'A pot of gold? Yes - How much will you take?' she says, but she don't look at him no more.

"'A pot of gold is at the end,' he says. 'This is the beginning, dear. . . . I want a promise.'

"'That would be a fair exchange, would it not?' she says, 'n' looks up at him. I never see eyes look like that before. They puts me in mind of when the band's playin' as the hosses go to the post fur the Kentucky Derby.

John Taintor Foote

"'Blister,' says Mr. Van, 'show the horses the view over the hill; they'll enjoy it.'

"I'm on my way in a hurry, but hears her say:

"'Oh, Billy, not here!'

"They don't come along fur half an hour. When they does, Mr. Van says to me:

"'Lead Rainbow to the Livingston stables, Blister. He has a new owner.'

"'Does you get a good price fur him?' I says, like I don't tumble to nothin'.

"'What a remarkable groom!' says Miss Livingston.

"'Isn't he?' says Mr. Van. Then he comes 'n' grabs me by the mitt. 'Don't worry about the price, old boy,' he says. 'No horse ever brought so much before!'"

SALVATION

At the invitation of Blister Jones I had come from the city's heat to witness the morning "work-outs". For two hours horse after horse had shot by, leaving a golden dust-cloud to hang and drift and slowly settle.

It was fairly cool under the big tree by the track fence, and the click of Blister's stop-watch, with his varied comments on what those clicks recorded, drifted out of my consciousness much as had the dust-clouds. Even the thr-rump, thr-rump, thr-rump of flying hoofs - crescendo, fortissimo, diminuendo - finally became meaningless.

"Here's one bred to suit you!" rasped a nasal voice, and I sat up, half awake, to observe a tall man lead a thorough-bred on to the track and dexterously "throw" a boy into the tiny saddle.

"Why?" Blister questioned.

"He's by Salvation," explained the tall man. "Likely-lookin' colt, ain't he? Think he favors the old hoss any?"

"'Bout the head he does," Blister answered. "He won't girt as big as the old hoss did at the same age."

"Well, if he's half as good as his daddy he's some hoss at that," the tall man stated, as he started up the track, watch in hand.

Blister followed the colt with his eyes.

John Taintor Foote

"Ever hear of Salvation?" he finally asked.

"Oh, yes," I replied.

"Well, I brings out Salvation as a three-year-old, 'n' what happens is quite a bunch of chatter - want to hear it?"

"You know it," I said, dropping into Blister's vernacular.

"That's pretty good for you," he said, grinning at my slang. "Well, to begin with, I'm in Loueyville. It's in the fall, 'n' I'm just back from Sheepshead. One way 'n' another I've had a good year. I'm down on two or three live ones when the odds are right, 'n' I've grabbed off a bundle I ain't ashamed to flash in any kind of company.

"My string's been shipped South, 'n' I thinks I'll knock around Kentucky fur a couple of weeks, 'n' see if I can't pick up some hosses to train.

"One mawnin' I'm in the Gait House, lookin' fur a hossman that's stoppin' there, 'n' I see Peewee Simpson settin' in the lobby like he'd just bought the hotel.

"'Who left the door open?' I says to him.

"'It's still open, I see,' says Peewee, lookin' at me.

"We exchanges a few more remarks, 'n' then Peewee tells me he's come to Loueyville to buy some yearlin's fur ole man Harris.

"'There's a dispersal sale to-morrow at the Goodloe farm,' says Peewee. "'N' I hear there's some real nice stuff going under the hammer. General Goodloe croaked this spring. They cleaned him in a cotton deal last year 'n' now their goin' to sell the whole works - studs, brood mares, colts - everything; plows, too - you want a plow? All you need is a plow 'n' a mule to put you where you belong.'

"'Where's this farm at?' I says.

"'Over in Franklin County,' says Peewee. 'I'm goin' over - want to go 'long?'

"'You're on,' I says. 'I'm not particular who travels with me any more.'

"We gets off the train next mawnin' at a little burg called Goodloe, 'n' there's three or four niggers with three or four ratty-lookin' ole rigs to drive hossmen out to the sale. It's a fierce drive, 'n' the springs is busted on our rig. I thinks we'll never get there, 'n' I begins to cuss Peewee fur bringin' me.

"'What you got to kick at?' says Peewee. 'Ain't you gettin' a free ride? Cheer up - think of all the nice plows you're goin' to see.'

"'You take them plows to hell 'n' make furrows in the cinders with 'em,' I says, wonderin' if I can get a train back to Loueyville anyways soon.

"But when we gets to the farm I'm glad I come. Man, that was some farm! Miles of level blue-grass pasture, with white fences cuttin' it up into squares, barns 'n' paddocks 'n' sheds, all painted white, just scattered around by the dozen. There's a track to work hosses on, too, but it's pretty much growed up with weeds. The main house is back in some big trees. It's brick 'n' has two porches, one on top of the other, all the way around it.

"The sale is just startin' when we get there. The auctioneer is in the judge's stand at the track 'n' the hosses is showed in the stretch.

"The first thing to sell is brood mares, 'n' they're as good a lot as I ever looks over. I loses Peewee in the crowd, 'n' climbs on to a shed roof to see better.

"Pretty soon here comes a real ole nigger leadin' a mare that looks to be about as old as the nigger. At that she showed class. Her head's still fine, 'n' her legs ain't got so much as a pimple on 'em.

"'Number eleven in your catalogues, gentlemen!' says the auctioneer. 'Mary Goodloe by Victory, first dam Dainty Maid by - what's the use of tellin' you *her* breedin', you *all* know *her*! Gentlemen,' he says, 'how many of you can say you ever owned a Kentucky Derby winner? Well, here's your chance to own one! This mare won the derby in - er -

"'Eighty-three, suh - I saw her do it,' says a man with a white mustache.

"'Eighty-three, thank you, Colonel. You have a fine memory,' says the auctioneer. 'I saw her do it, too. Now, gentlemen,' he says, 'what am I offered for this grand old mare? She's the dam of six winners - three of 'em stake hosses. Kindly start the bidding.'

"'Twenty dollahs!' says the ole nigger who has hold of the mare.

"'Fifty!' says some one else.

"'Hole on dah,' sings out the ole nigger. 'I'se just 'bliged to tell you folks I'se pu'chasin' dis hyar mare fo' Miss Sally Goodloe!'

"The auctioneer looks at the guy who bids fifty.

"'I withdraw that bid,' says the guy.

"'Sold to you for twenty dollars, Uncle Jake,' says the auctioneer. 'Bring on number twelve!'

"'Hyah's yo' twenty dollahs,' says the ole nigger, fishin' out a roll of raggedy bills and passin' 'em up to the stand.

"'Thank you, Uncle Jake. Come to the clerk for your bill of sale this evenin',' says the auctioneer.

"I watches the sale a while longer, 'n' then mooches into the big barn where the yearlin's 'n' two-year-olds is waitin' to be sold. They're a nice lot of colts, but I ain't interested in this young stuff - colts is too much of a gamble fur me. Only about one in fifty'll make good. Somebody else can spend their money on 'em at that kind of odds.

"I goes out of the colt barn 'n' begins to ramble around, lampin' things in general. I comes to a shed full of plows, 'n' I has to laugh when I sees 'em. I'm standin' there with a grin on my face when a nigger comes 'round the shed 'n' sees me lookin' at them plows.

"'Fine plows, sah, an' vehy cheap,' he says.

"'Do I look like I needs a plow?' I says to him.

"'No, sah,' says the nigger, lookin' me over. 'I cyant rightly say you favohs plowin', but howkum you ain' tendin' de sale?'

"'I don't see nothin' over there that suits me,' I says.

"The nigger is sore in a minute.

"'You is suttanly hahd to please, white man,' he says. 'Ain' no finah colts in Kaintucky dan dem.'

"'That may be so, but how about Tennessee?' I says, just to get him goin'.

"'Tennessee! Tennessee!' he says. 'What you talkin' 'bout? Why, *we* does de fahm wuck wid likelier colts dan *dey* sends to de races.'

"'I've seed some nifty babies down there,' I says.

"'Look-a-hyar, man!' he says, 'you want to see a colt what am a colt?'

"'How far?' I says.

"'No ways at all, jus' over yondah,' says the nigger.

"'Lead me to it,' I say to him, 'n' he takes me over to a long lane with paddocks down each side of it. All the paddocks is empty but two. In the first one is the ole mare, Mary Goodloe; 'n' next to her is a slashin' big chestnut colt.

"'Cast yo' eyes on dat one!' says the nigger.

"I don't say nothin' fur five minutes. I just looks at that colt. I never sees one like him before, nor since. There's some dead leaves blowin' around the paddock 'n' he's jumpin' on 'em with his front feet like a setter pup playin'. Two jumps 'n' he's clear across the paddock! His shoulders 'n' quarters 'n' legs is made to order. His head 'n' throat-latch is clean as a razor, 'n' he's the proudest thing that ever stood on four legs. He looks to be comin' three, but he's muscled like a five-year-old.

"'How 'bout him, boss?' says the nigger after a while.

"'Well,' I says, 'they broke the mold when they made that one!'

"'Dar's de mold,' he says, pointin' to the ole mare in the next paddock. 'She's his mammy. Dat's Mahey Goodloe, named fo' ole Miss Goodloe what's dade. Dat mare win de derby. Dis hyar colt's by impo'ted Calabash.'

"'When does this colt sell?' I asks him.

"'He ain' fo' sale,' says the nigger. 'De estate doan own him. De General done gib him to Miss Sally when de colt's bohn.'

"'Where's she at now?' I says to the nigger. I had to own that colt if my roll could reach him - I knowed that 'fore I'd looked at him a minute.

"'Up to de house, mos' likely,' says the nigger. 'You'd better save yo' shoe leather, boss. She ain' gwine to sell dat colt no matter what happens.'

"I beats it up to the big house, but when I gets there I see nobody's livin' in it. The windows has boards across 'em. I looks in between the cracks 'n' sees a whale of a room. Hangin' from the ceilin' is two things fur lights all covered with glass dingles. They ain't nothin' else in the room but a tall mirror, made of gold, that goes clear to the ceilin'. I walks clean around the house, but it's sure empty, so I oozes back to the barns 'n' collars the sales clerk.

"'I'm a-lookin' fur Miss Goodloe,' I tells him. 'A nigger says she's at the house, but I've just been up there 'n' they ain't even furniture in it.'

"'No,' says the clerk; 'the furniture was sold to a New York collector two weeks ago. Miss Goodloe is livin' in the head trainer's house across the road yonder. She won't have that long, I don't reckon, though I did hear she's fixin' to buy it when the farm sells, with some money ole Mrs. Goodloe left her.'

"I goes over to the little house the clerk points out, 'n' knocks. A right fat nigger woman, with her sleeves rolled up, comes to the door.

"'What you want?' she says.

"'I want to see Miss Goodloe,' I says.

"'You cyant see her. She ain' seein' nobody,' says the nigger woman, 'n' starts to shut the door.

"'Wait a minute, aunty," I says. 'I got to see her - it's business, sure-enough business.'

"'Doan you aunty me!' says she. 'Now, you take yo' bisniss with you an' ramble! Bisniss has done sole off eve'y stick an' stone we got! I doan want to hyar no mo' 'bout bisniss long as I live' - 'n' bang goes the door.

"I waits a minute 'n' then knocks again - nothin' doin'. I knocks fur five minutes steady. Pretty soon here she comes, but this time she's got a big brass-handled poker with her.

"'Ef I has to clout you ovah de haid wid dis pokah you ain' gwine to transack no mo' bisniss fo' a tollable long time!' she says. She's mad all right, 'n' she hollers this at me pretty loud.

"'Fore I can say anythin' a dame steps out in the hall 'n' looks at me 'n' the nigger woman 'n' the poker.

"'What's the matter, Liza?' she says to the nigger woman, 'n' her voice is good to listen at. You don't care what she says, just so she keeps a-sayin' it. She's got on a white dress with black fixin's on it, 'n' she just suits her dress, 'cause her hair is dark 'n' her face is white, 'n' she has great big eyes that put me in mind of - I don't know what! She ain't very tall, but she makes me feel littler'n her when she looks at me. She's twenty-four or five, mebby, but I'm a bum guesser at a dame's age.

"'Dis pusson boun' he gwine to see you an' I boun' he ain', Miss Sally,' says the nigger woman. The little dame comes out on the porch.

"'I am Miss Goodloe,' she says to me. 'What do you wish?'

"'I want to buy a hoss from you, ma'am,' I says to her.

"'The horses are being sold across the way at that biggest barn,' she says.

"'Yes'm,' I says, 'I've just come from there. I -'

"'Have you been watching the sale?' she says, breakin' in.

"'Yes'm - some,' I says.

"'Liza, you may go to your kitchen now,' she says. 'Can you tell me if they have sold the mare, Mary Goodloe, yet?' she says to me when the nigger woman's gone.

"'Yes'm, she was sold,' I says.

"She flinches like I'd hit her 'n' I see her chin begin to quiver, but she bites her lip 'n' I looks off down the road to give her a chance. Pretty soon she's back fur more. I'm feelin' like a hound.

"'Do you know who bought her?' she says.

"'A nigger man they call Uncle Jake buys her,' I says.

"'Uncle Jake!' she says. 'Are you sure? Was he an old man with poor eyesight?'

"'He was old all right,' I says. 'But I don't notice about his eyes. He give twenty dollars fur her.'

"'Is that all she brought?' she says.

"'Well, she brings more,' I says, 'only the ole man makes a speech 'n' tells 'em he's buying her fur you. Everybody quit biddin' then.' She stands there a minute, her eyes gettin' bigger 'n' bigger. I never see eyes so big 'n' soft 'n' dark.

"'Would you do me a favor?' she says at last.

"'Fifty of 'em,' I says. She gives me a little smile.

"'One's all that's necessary, thank you,' she says. 'Will you find Uncle Jake for me and tell him I wish to see him?'

"'You bet I will,' I says, 'n' I beats it over to the barns. . . I finds Uncle Jake, 'n' he's got weak eyes all right - he can't

John Taintor Foote

hardly see. He's got rheumatism, too - he's all crippled up with it. When I gets back with him, Miss Goodloe's still standin' on the porch.

"'I want to find out who bought old Mary, Uncle Jake,' she says. 'Do you know?'

"'I was jus' fixin' to come over hyar an' tell you de good news, Miss Sally,' says Uncle Jake. 'When dey puts ole Mahey up to' sale, she look pow'ful ole an' feeble. De autioneer jes 'seeches 'em fo' to make some sawt o' bid, but hit ain' no use. Dey doan' nobody want her. Hit look lak de auctioneer in a bad hole - he doan' know what to do zakly. Hit's gittin' mighty 'bahassin' fo' him, so I say to him: "Mr. Auctioneer, I ain' promisin' nothin', but Miss Sally Goodloe mought be willin' to keep dis hyar ole mare fo' 'membrance sake." De auctioneer am mighty tickled, an' he say, "Uncle Jake, ef Miss Sally will 'soom de 'sponsibility ob dis ole mare, hit would 'blige me greatly." Dat's howkum ole Mahey back safe in de paddock, an' dey ain' *nobody* gwine to take her away fum you, honey!'

"'Uncle Jake,' says Miss Goodloe, 'where is your twenty dollars you got for that tobacco you raised?'

"'Ain' I tole you 'bout dat, Miss Sally? Dat mis'able money done skip out an' leave thoo a hole in ma pocket,' says Uncle Jake, 'n' pulls one of his pants pockets inside out. Sure enough, there's a big hole in it.

"'Didn't I give you a safety-pin to pin that money in your inside coat pocket?' says Miss Goodloe.

"'Yess'm, dat's right,' he says. 'But I'se countin' de money one day an' a span ob mules broke loose an' stahts lickety-brindle fo' de bahn, an' aimin' to ketch de mules, I pokes de money in de pocket wid de hole. I ain' neber see dat no-'coun' money sence.'

"Miss Goodloe looks at the ole nigger fur a minute.

"'Uncle Jake . . . oh, Uncle Jake . . .' she says. '*These* are the things I just *can't* stand!' Her eyes fill up, 'n' while she bites her lip agin, it ain't no use. Two big tears roll down her cheeks. 'I'll see you in a moment,' she says to me, 'n' goes inside.

"'Bad times! Bad times, pow'ful bad times!' says Uncle Jake, 'n' hobbles away a-mutterin' to hisself.

"It's begun to get under my skin right. I'm feelin' queer, 'n' I gets to thinkin' I'd better beat it. 'Don't be a damn fool!' I says to myself. 'You ain't had nothin' to do with the cussed business 'n' you can't help it none. If you don't buy this colt somebody else will.' So I sets on the edge of the porch 'n' waits. It ain't so long till Miss Goodloe comes out again. I gets up 'n' takes off my hat.

"'What horse do you wish to buy?' she says.

"'A big chestnut colt by Calabash, dam Mary Goodloe,' I says. 'They tell me you own him.'

"'Oh, I *can't* sell *him*!' she says, backin' towards the door. 'No one has ever ridden him but me.'

"'Is he fast?' I asks her.

"'Of course,' she says.

"'Is he mannered?' I asks.

"'Perfectly,' she says.

"'He ain't never seen a barrier, I suppose?' I says.

"'He's broken to the barrier,' she says then.

"'Who schools him?' I says. 'You tells me nobody's been on him but you -'

John Taintor Foote

"'I schooled him at the barrier with the other two-year-olds,' she says.

"'Whee!' I says. 'You must be able to ride some.'

"'I'd be ashamed of myself if I couldn't,' she says.

"'Are you sure you won't sell him?' I asks her.

"'Positive,' she says, 'n' I see she means it.

"'What you goin' to do with him?' I says. 'Don't you know it's wicked not to give that colt a chance to show what he can do?'

"'I know it is,' she says. 'But I have no money for training expenses.'

"I studies a minute, 'n' all of a sudden it comes to me. 'You were just achin' to help this little dame a while ago,' I says to myself. 'Here's a chance . . . be a sport!' The colt *might* make good, 'n' she could use a thousand or so awful easy.

"'Miss Goodloe,' I says out loud, 'I might as well tell you I'm in love with that colt.' She gives me a real sweet smile.

"'Isn't he a darling?' she says, her face lightin' up.

"'That isn't the way I'd put it,' I says, 'but I guess we mean the same. Now, I'm a race-hoss trainer. You read these letters from people I'm workin' fur, 'n' then I'll tell you what I want to do.' I fishes out a bunch of letters from my pocket 'n' she sets down on the steps 'n' begins to read 'em solemn as owls.

"'Why do they call you Blister?' she asks, lookin' up from a letter.

"'That's a nickname,' I says.

"'Oh,' she says, 'n' goes on readin'. When she gets through she hands the letters to me. 'They seem to have a lot of confidence in you, Blis - Mr. Jones,' she says.

"'Stick to Blister,' I says, "'n' I'll always come when I'm called.'

"'Very well, Blister,' she says. 'Now, why did you wish me to read those letters?'

"'I asks you to read them letters, because I got a hunch that colt's a winner, 'n' I want to take a chance on him,' I says. 'I got a string of hosses at New Awlins - now, you let me ship that colt down there 'n' I'll get him ready. I'll charge you seventy-five a month to be paid out his winnings. If he don't win - no charge. Is it a go?' She don't say nothin' fur quite a while. 'I sees a dozen hossmen I knows over at the sale,' I says. 'If you want recommends I can get any of 'em to come over 'n' speak to you about me.'

"'No, I feel that you are trustworthy,' she says, 'n' goes to studyin' some more. 'What I should like to know,' she says after while, 'is this: Do trainers make a practise of taking horses at the same terms you have just offered me?'

"'Sure they do,' I lies, lookin' her in the eye. 'Any trainer'll take a chance on a promisin' colt.'

"'Are you certain?' she asks me, earnest.

"'Yes'm, dead certain,' I says. She don't say nothin' fur maybe five minutes, then she gets up 'n' looks at me steady.

"'You may take him,' she says, 'n' walks into the house.

"I finds Uncle Jake 'n' eases him two bucks. It sure helps his rheumatism. He gets as spry as a two-year-old. He tells me there's a train at nine that evenin'. I sends him to the depot to fix it so I can take the colt to Loueyville in the express car, 'n' he says he'll get back quick as he can. I hunts up Peewee, but he's goin' to stay all night, 'cause the yearlin's won't sell till

John Taintor Foote

next day. . . .

"The sun's goin' down when we starts fur the depot, Uncle Jake drivin', 'n' me settin' behind, leadin' the colt. The sunlight's red, 'n' when it hits that chestnut colt he shines like copper. Say, but he was some proud peacock!

"I sends word to Miss Goodloe we're comin', 'n' she's waitin' at the gate. The colt nickers when he sees her, 'n' she comes 'n' takes the lead strap from me. Then she holds up her finger at the colt.

"'Now, Boy-baby!' she says. 'Everything depends on you - you're all mammy has in the world . . . will you do your best for her sake?' The colt paws 'n' arches his neck. 'See, he says he will!' she says to me.

"'What's his name?' I asks her.

"'Oh, dear, he hasn't any!' she says. 'I've always called him Boy-baby.'

"'He can't race under that,' I says.

"'Between now and the time he starts I'll think of a name for him,' she says. 'Do you really believe he can win?'

"'They tell me his dam wins twenty thousand the first year she raced,' I says.

"'He'd be our salvation if he did that,' she says.

"'There's a name,' I says. 'Call him Salvation!' She says over it two or three times.

"'That's not a bad racing name, is it?' she asks me.

"'No'm,' I says. 'That's a good name.'

"'Very well, Boy-baby,' she says to the colt. 'I christen thee *Salvation*, with this lump of sugar. That's a fine name! Always bear it bravely.' She puts her arms around the colt's neck 'n' kisses him on the nose. Then she hands me the lead strap 'n' steps aside. 'Good-by, and good luck!' she says.

"When we turns the bend, way down the road, she's still standin' there watchin' us . . .

"I sends the colt down with a swipe, 'n' he's been at the track a week when I gets to New Awlins. The boys have begun to talk 'bout him already, he's such a grand looker. He don't give me no trouble at all. He's quiet 'n' kind 'n' trustin'. Nothin' gets him excited, 'n' I begins to be afraid he'll be a sluggard. It don't take me long to see he won't do fur the sprints - distance is what he likes. He's got a big swingin' gallop that sure fools me at first. He never seems to be tryin' a lick. When he's had two months prep. I has my exercise-boy let him down fur a full mile. Man! he *just gallops* in *forty flat!* Then I know I've got somethin'!

"His first race I'm as nervous as a dame. I don't bet a dollar on him fur fear I'll queer it. Anyway, he ain't a good price - you can't keep him under cover, he's too flashy-lookin'.

"Well, he comes home alone, just playin' along, the jock lookin' back at the bunch.

"'How much has he got left?' I says to the jock after the race.

"'Him!' says the jock. 'Enough to beat anybody's hoss!'

"I starts him the next week, 'n' he repeats, but it ain't till his *third* race that I know fur sure he's a great hoss, with a racin' heart.

"Sweeney has the mount, 'n' he don't get him away good - the colt's layin' a bad seventh at the quarter. Banjo's out in front, away off - 'n' she's a real good mare. That pin-head Sweeney don't make a move till the stretch, then he tries to come from seventh all at once . . . 'n' by God, he does it! That colt comes from nowhere to the Banjo mare while they're goin' an eighth! The boy on Banjo goes to the bat, but the colt just gallops on by 'n' breezes in home.

"'You bum!' I says to Sweeney. 'What kind of a trip do you call that? Did you get off 'n' shoot a butsy at the stretch bend?'

"'If I has a match I would,' says Sweeney. 'I kin smoke it easy, 'n' then *back* in ahead of them turtles.'

"I know then the colt's good enough fur the stakes, 'n' I writes Miss Goodloe to see if I can use the fourteen hundred he's won to make the first payments. She's game as a pebble, 'n' says to stake him the limit. So I enters him from New Awlins to Pimlico.

"I've had all kinds of offers fur the colt, but I always tell 'em nothin' doin'. One day a lawyer named Jack Dillon, who owns a big stock farm near Lexington, comes to me 'n' says he wants to buy him.

"'He ain't fur sale,' I tells him.

"'Everything's for sale at a price,' he says. 'Now I want that colt worse than I do five thousand. What do you say?'

"'I ain't sayin' nothin',' I says.

"'How does eight thousand look to you?' he says.

"'Big,' I says. 'But you'll have to see Miss Goodloe at Goodloe, Kentucky, if you want this colt.'

"Oh, General Goodloe's daughter,' he says. 'Does she own him? When I go back next week I'll drop over and see her.'

"Well, Salvation starts in the Crescent City Derby, 'n' when he comes under the wire Miss Goodloe's five thousand bucks better off. He wins another stake, 'n' then I ship him with the rest of my string to Nashville. The second night we're there, here comes Jack Dillon to the stall with a paper bag in his hand.

"'You didn't get the colt?' I says to him.

"'No,' he says. 'I didn't get anything . . . I lost something.'

"'What?' I says.

"'Never mind what,' he says. 'Here, put this bag of sugar where I can get at it. She told me to feed him two lumps a day.'

"After that he comes every evenin' 'n' gives the colt sugar, but he's poor company. He just stands lookin' at the colt. Half the time he don't hear what I say to him.

"The colt wins the Nashville Derby, 'n' then I ships him to Loueyville for the Kentucky. We want him to win *that* more'n all the rest, but as luck goes, he ketches cold shippin', 'n' he can't start.

"Miss Goodloe comes over to Loueyville one mawnin' to see him. She gets through huggin' him after while, 'n' sets down in a chair by the stall door.

"'Now, start at the beginning and tell me everything,' she says.

"So I tells her every move the colt makes since I has him.

"'How did he happen to catch cold?' she asks.

"'Constitution undermined,' I says.

"'Oh! How dreadful!' she says. 'What caused it?'

"'Sugar,' I says, never crackin' a smile.

"She flushes up, 'n' I see she knows what I mean, but she don't ask no more questions. Before she leaves, Miss Goodloe tells me she'll come to Cincinnati if the colt's well enough to start in the Latonia Derby.

"I ships to Cincinnati. About noon derby day I'm watchin' the swipes workin' on the colt. He's favorite fur the Latonia 'n' there's mebby a hundred boobs in front of the stall rubberin' at him.

"'Please let dis lady pass,' I hears some one say, 'n' here comes Liza helpin' Miss Goodloe through the crowd. When Liza sees me I ducks 'n' holds up my arm like I'm dodgin' somethin'. She grins till her mouth looks like a tombstone factory.

"'I clean fohgot to bring dat pokah wid me,' she says. 'Hyar you is, Miss Sally.'

"I don't hardly know Miss Goodloe. There's nothin' like race day to get a dame goin'. Her eyes are shinin' 'n' her cheeks are pink, 'n' she don't look more'n sixteen.

"'Why, Boy-baby,' she says to the colt, 'you've grown to be such a wonderful person I can't believe it's you!' The colt knows it's race day 'n' he don't pay much attention to her. 'Oh, Boy-baby!' says Miss Goodloe, 'I'm afraid you've had your head turned . . . you don't even notice your own mammy!'

"'His head ain't turned, it's full of race,' I says to her. He'll come down to earth after he gets that mile-'n'-a-quarter under his belt.'

"When the bugle blows, Miss Goodloe asks me to stay in her box with her while the derby's run. There's twenty thousand people there 'n' I guess the whole bunch has bet on the colt, from the way it sounds when the hosses parade past. You can't hear nothin' but 'Salva-a-tion! Oh, you Salva-a-tion!'

"They get a nice break all in a line, but when they come by the stand the first time, the colt's layin' at the rail a len'th in front, fightin' fur his head.

"'*Salva-a-tion*!' goes up from the stands in one big yell.

"'*There he goes*!' hollers some swipe across the track, 'n' then everything is quiet.

"Miss Goodloe's got her fingers stuck into my arm till it hurts. But that don't bother me.

"'Isn't it wonderful?' she says, but the pink's gone out of her cheeks. She's real pale . . .

"They never get near the colt. . . . He comes home alone with that big easy, swingin' gallop of his, 'n' goes under the wire still fightin' fur his head.

"Then that crowd goes plumb crazy! Men throws their hats away, 'n' dances around, yellin' till they can't whisper! Miss Goodloe is shakin' so I has to hold her up.

"'Isn't he *grand*? How would you like to own him?' a woman in the next box says to her.

"'I'd love it,' says Miss Goodloe, 'n' busts out cryin'. 'You'll think I'm an awful baby!' she says to me.

"'I don't mind them kind of tears,' I says.

"'Neither do I,' she says, laughin', 'n' dabbin' at her face with a dinky little hankerchiff.

"I wait till they lead the colt out in front of the stand, 'n' put the floral horseshoe round his neck, then I takes Miss Goodloe down to shake hands with the jock.

"'How do you like him?' she says to the jock.

"'Well, ma'am,' he says, 'I've ridden all the good ones, but he's the best hoss I ever has under me!'

"'What's the record fur this race?' I yells across the track to the timer. He points down at the time hung up.

"'That's it!' he hollers back.

"'Didn't he do it easy?' says the jock to me.

"There's no use to tell you what Salvation done to them Eastern hosses; everybody knows about that. It got so the ginnies would line up in a bunch, every time he starts, 'n' holler: '*They're off - there he goes!*' They does it regular, 'n' pretty soon the crowds get next 'n' then everybody does it. He begins to stale off at Pimlico, so I ships him to Miss Goodloe, 'n' writes her to turn him out fur three or four months.

"It ain't a year from the time we leaves Miss Goodloe standin' in the road till then. Salvation wins his every start. He's copped off forty thousand bucks. I guess that's goin' some!

"When the season closes I goes through Kentucky on my way South, 'n' I takes a jump over from Loueyville to see the colt. Miss Goodloe's bought a hundred acres around her little house, 'n' the colt's turned out in a nice bluegrass field. We're standin' watchin' him, when she puts somethin' in my pocket. I fishes it out 'n' it's a check fur five thousand bucks.

"'I've been paid what's comin' to me,' I says. 'Nothin' like this goes.'

"'Oh, yes, it does!' she says. 'I have investigated since you told me that *story*. Trainers do *not* pay expenses on other people's horses. Now, put that back in your pocket or I will be mortally offended.'

"'I don't need it,' I says.

"'Neither do I,' she says. 'I haven't told you - guess what I've been offered for Salvation?'

"'I give it up,' I says.

"'Fifty thousand dollars,' she says. 'What do you think of that?'

"'Are you goin' to sell?' I asks her.

"'Certainly not,' she says.

"'He'll earn twice that in the stud,' I says. 'Who makes you the offer - Mr. Dillon?'

"'No, a New York man,' she says. 'I guess Mr. Dillon has lost interest in him.'

"I guess he hasn't,' I says. 'I seen him at Pimlico, 'n' he was worse 'n ever.'

"'Did - did he still feed him sugar?' she says, but she don't look at me while she's gettin' it out.

"'You bet he did,' I says.

"'Shall you see him again?' she asks me.

"'Yes'm, I'll see him at New Awlins,' I says.

"'You may tell him,' she says, her face gettin' pink, 'that as far as my horse is concerned I haven't changed my mind.'

"On the way back to the house I gets to thinkin'.

"'I'm goin' round to the kitchen 'n' say hello to Aunt Liza,' I says to Miss Goodloe.

"Liza's glad to see me this time - mighty glad.

"'Hyah's a nice hot fried cake fo' you, honey,' she says.

"'This ain't no fried cake,' I says. 'This is a doughnut.'

"'You ain' tryin' to tell *me* what a fried cake is, is you?' she says.

"'Aunt Liza,' I says to her while I'm eatin' the doughnut, 'I sees Mr. Jack Dillon after he's been here, 'n' he acts like he'd had a bad time. Did you take a poker to him, too?'

"'No, sah,' she says. 'Miss Sally tended to his case.'

"'It's too bad she don't like him,' I says.

"'Who say she doan' like him?' says Liza. 'He come a sto'min' round hyah like he gwine to pull de whole place up by de roots an' transport hit ovah Lexington way. Fust he's boun' fo' to take dat hoss what's done win all dem good dollahs. Den his min' flit f'om dat to Miss Sally, an' he's aimin' to cyar her off like she was a 'lasses bar'l or a yahd ob calico. Who is dem Dillons, anyway? De Goodloes owned big lan' right hyar in Franklin County when de Dillons ain' nothin' but Yankee trash back in Maine or some other outlan'ish place! Co'se we sends him 'bout his bisniss - him an' his money! Ef he comes roun' hyar, now we's rich again, an' sings small fo' a while. Miss Sally mighty likely to listen to what he got to say - she so kindly dat a-way.'

"At the depot in Goodloe that night I writes a wire to Jack Dillon. 'If you still want Salvation better come to Goodloe,' is what the wire says. I signs it 'n' sends it 'n' takes the train fur New Awlins.

"The colt ruptures a tendon not long after that, so he never races no more, 'n' I ain't never been to Goodloe since."

Blister yawned, lay back on the grass and pulled his hat over his face.

"Is Salvation alive now?' I asked.

"Sure he's alive!" The words come muffled from beneath the hat. "He's at the head of Judge Dillon's stock farm over near Lexington."

"I'm surprised Miss Goodloe sold him," I said.

"She don't . . . sell him," Blister muttered drowsily. "Mrs. Dillon . . . still . . . owns him."

John Taintor Foote

A TIP IN TIME

Blister was silent as we left the theater. I had chosen the play because I had fancied it would particularly appeal to him. The name part - a characterization of a race-horse tout - had been acceptably done by a competent young actor. The author had hewn as close to realism as his too clever lines would permit. There had been a wealth of Blister's own vernacular used on the stage during the evening, and I had rather enjoyed it all. But Blister, it was now evident, had been disappointed.

"You didn't like it?" I said tentatively, as I steered him toward the blazing word "Rathskeller," a block down the street.

"Oh, I've seed worse shows," was the unenthusiastic reply. "I can get an earful of that kind of chatter dead easy without pryin' myself loose from any kale," he added.

I saw where the trouble lay. The terse expressive jargon of the race track, its dry humor just beneath its hard surface, might delight the unsophisticated, but not Blister. To him it lacked in novelty.

"I ain't been in one of these here rats ketchers fur quite a while," said Blister, as we descended the steps beneath the flambuoyant sign. "Do you go to shows much?" he asked, when two steins were between us on the flemish oak board.

"Not a great deal," I replied. "I did dramatics - wrote up shows - for two years and that rather destroyed my enjoyment of the theater."

"I got you," said Blister. "Seein' so much of it spoils you fur it. That's me, too. I won't cross the street to see a show when I'm on the stage."

Had he suddenly announced himself king of the Cannibal Islands I would have looked and felt about as then. I gazed at him with dropping jaw.

"No, I ain't bugs!" he grinned, as he saw my expression. "I'm on the stage quite a while. Ain't I never told you?"

"You certainly have not," I said emphatically.

"I goes on the stage just because I starts to cuss a dog I owns one day," said Blister. "It's the year they pull off one of these here panic things, and believe me the kale just fades from view! It you borrow a rub-rag, three ginnies come along to bring it back when you're through. If you happens to mention you ain't got your makin's with you, the nearest guy to you'll call the police. They wouldn't have a hoss trained that could run a mile in nothin'.

"A dog out on grass don't cost but two bucks a month. It seems like the men I'm workin' fur all remembers this at once. When I'm through followin' shippin' instructions I'm down to one mutt, 'n' I owns him myself. He's some hoss - I don't think. He's got a splint big as a turkey egg that keeps him ouchy in front half the time, 'n' his heart ain't in the right place. I've filled his old hide so full of hop you could knock his eyes off with a club, tryin' to make him cop, but he won't come through - third is the best he'll do.

"One day about noon I'm standin' lookin' in the stall door, watchin' him mince over his oats. They ain't nothin' good about this dog - not even his appetite. I ain't had a real feed myself fur three days, 'n' when I sees this ole counterfeit mussin' over his grub I opens up on him.

John Taintor Foote

"'Why, you last year's bird's nest!' I says to him. 'What th' hell right have you got to be fussy with your eats? They ain't a oat in that box but what out-classes you - they've all growed faster'n you can run! The only thing worse'n you is a ticket on you to win. If I pulls your shoes off 'n' has my choice between you 'n' them - I takes the shoes. If I wouldn't be pinched fur it I gives you to the first nut they lets out of the bughouse - you sour-bellied-mallet-headed-yellow pup! You cross between a canary 'n' a mud-turtle!'

"That gets me sort-a warmed up, 'n' then I begins to really tell this dog what the sad sea waves is sayin'. When I can't think of nothin'
more to call him, I stops.

"'Outside of that he's all right, ain't he?' says some one behind me.

"'No,' I says, 'he has other faults besides.'

"I turns round 'n' there's a fat guy with a cigar in his face. He's been standin' there listenin'. He's got a chunk of ice stuck in his chest that you have to look at through smoked glasses. He's got another one just as big on his south hook. Take him all 'n' all he looks like the real persimmon.

"'Do you own him?' says the fat guy.

"'You've had no call to insult a stranger,' I says. 'But it's on me - I owns him.'

"'I'm sorry you've got such a bad opinion of him,' he says. 'I was thinkin' of buyin' him.'

"I looks around fur this guy's keeper - they ain't nobody in sight.

"'This ain't such a bad hoss,' I says. 'Them remarks you hears don't mean nothin'. They're my regular pet names fur him.'

"'I'd like to be around once when you talk to a bad one,' says the guy. 'Now look a-here,' he says. 'I'll buy this horse, but get over all thoughts of makin' a sucker out of me. What do you want for him? If you try to stick me up - I'm gone. The woods is full of this kind. Let's hear from you!'

"'Fur a hundred I throws in a halter,' I says.

"'You've sold one,' says the guy, 'n' peels off five yellow men from a big roll.

"When I've got the kale safe in my clothes, I gets curious.

"'What do you want with this hoss?' I says.

"'He's to run on rollers in a racing scene,' he says.

"'Well,' I says, 'some skates has rollers on 'em, maybe they'll help this one. God knows he ain't any good with just legs!'

"'He's plenty good enough for his act,' says the guy. 'And say, I want another one like him, and a man to go on the road with 'em. Can you put me wise?'

"'How much would be crowded towards the party you want, Saturday nights?' I says.

"'Twenty dollars and expenses,' says he.

"'Make it thirty,' I says. 'Travelin's hard on them that loves their home.'

"'We'll split it,' he says. 'Twenty-five's the word.'

"'My time's yours,' I says.

"'How about the other horse?' says the fat guy.

"'You'll own him in eight minutes,' I says. 'Stay here with

Edwin Booth till I get back.'

"I hustles down the line 'n' finds Peewee Simpson washin' out bandages - that's what he'd come to.

"'You still got that sorrel hound?' I says to him.

"'Nope,' says Peewee. 'He's got me. I'm takin' in washin' to support him.'

"'Brace yourself fur a shock,' I says. 'I'll give you real money fur him.'

"Peewee looks at me fur a minute like you done a while ago.

"'Don't wake me up!' he says. 'I must - ' then he stops 'n' takes another slant at me. 'Say!' he says, 'I'll bet you've got next! I ain't told you yet - who put you hep?'

"'Hep to what?' I says.

"'Why, this hoss works a mile in forty yesterday,' says Peewee. 'I'm goin' to cop with him next week.'

"'Your work's coarse,' I says. 'The only way that dog goes a mile in forty is in the baggage coach ahead. I'm in a hurry! Here's a hundred fur the pup. Don't break a leg gettin' him out of the stall.'

"I don't stop to answer Peewee's questions, but leads the hoss back to the fat guy.

"'Here's Salvini,' I says. 'He cost you a hundred.'

"'S. R. O. for you,' says he, 'n' slips me the hundred. 'Now, take him and Edwin Booth to the livery-stable round the corner from the Alhambra Theater. Come to the Gilsey House at six o'clock and ask for me. My name is Banks.'

"'There's class to that name,' I says. 'It sure sounds good to me.'

"'Keep on your toes like you've done so far and it'll be as good as it sounds,' says he.

"That evenin' Banks tells me the dogs he's bought is fur a show called *A Blue Grass Belle*. A dame is to ride one of 'em in the show, 'n' I'm to ride the other.

"'I've arranged to have the apparatus set up back of the livery-stable,' says Banks, 'so you can rehearse the horses for their act. When they know their parts I'll bring Pixley around and you can work the act together. She was a rube before she hit the big town and she says she can ride.'

"Say, this dingus fur the hosses to run on is there like a duck. The guy that thinks it up has a grand bean! You leads a hoss on to it 'n' when it's ready you gives him the word. He starts to walk off, nothin' doin', he ain't goin' nowhere. You fans him with the bat. 'I'll be on my way,' he says. But he ain't got a chance - the faster he romps the faster the dingus rolls out from under him. He can run a forty shot, 'n' he don't go no further 'n I can throw a piano!

"After I've worked both dogs on the dingus fur a week or so, I tells Banks they know the game - 'n' believe me, they did! Why, them ole hounds got so they begins to prance when they see the machine. They'd lay down 'n' ramble till they dropped if I lets 'em. They liked it fine!

"'I'll send Pixley around to-morrow,' says Banks. 'I want you to teach her the jockey's crouch when she's on her horse.'

"Next mawnin' I'm oilin' up the dingus when a chicken pokes her little head out the back door of the livery-stable.

"'Hello, kid,' she says to me.

John Taintor Foote

"'Hello, girlie,' I says back.

"'*Miss Pixley*, if you *please*,' she says.

"'All right,' I says. "N' while we're at it Mr. Jones'll suit me.'

"'Fade away,' she says, 'n' I see she's got a couple of dimples. 'Mr. Jones don't suit you.'

"'Make it Blister, then,' I says.

"'You're on,' she says. 'And you can stick to girlie.'

"Say, she was a great little dame; she makes a hit with me the first dash out of the box. When it comes to ridin' she's game as a wasp. She has on a long coat, 'n' I don't see what's underneath.

"'Banks tells me you ride like a jock in the show,' I says. 'You can't cut the mustard with that rig on.'

"'Sure not, Simple Simon!' she says. 'Do you think this grows on me?' She sheds the coat, 'n' I see she's got on leggins 'n' a pair of puffy pants.

"I throws her on to Salvini 'n' he begins to prance around, me holdin' him by the head.

"'Whoa, you big bum!' I says to him.

"'Quit knocking my horse,' she says. 'Let go of him and see if I care.'

"I turns him loose 'n' she lets him jump a few times 'n' then rides him on to the machine. I see she knows her business so I stands beside her 'n' makes her sit him like she ought. It don't take her no time to get wise. Pretty soon she's clear over with a hand on each side of his withers, 'n' him goin' like a stake hoss.

"'That's the dope!' I hollers. I has to yell 'cause the ole hound is makin' a fierce racket on the machine.

"'I feel like a monkey on a stick,' she hollers back, but she don't look like one. Her hair's shook loose, her eyes is shinin', 'n' them dimples of her's is the life of the party.

"'So long, professor,' she says to me when she's goin'. 'Much obliged for the lesson. Our act will be a scream.'

"Not long after that they moves the dingus over to the theater, 'n' Banks tells me to bring the hosses over at three o'clock the next day. I'm there to the minute, but nobody shows up 'n' I stands out in front with the dogs fur what seems like a week. All of a sudden a tall pale guy, who ain't got no coat on, comes bustin' out of the entrance.

"'Where in hell and damnation have you been with these skates?' he says. His hair is stickin' up on end 'n' he's got a wild look in his eye.

"'Batty as a barn,' I says to myself, 'n' gets behind Edwin Booth.

"'Speak up!' says the pale guy. 'Before I do murder!' I looks up 'n' down the street - not a cop in sight.

"'I'm a gone fawn skin,' I says to myself, but I thinks I'll try to soothe him till help comes.

"'That's all right, pal, that's all right,' I says to him. 'These pretty hosses are in a show. Did you ever see a show? I seen a show once that -'

"'My poor boy,' he says, breakin' in. 'I didn't know! What got into Banks?' he says, sort-a to hisself. 'Try and remember,' he says to me, 'weren't you told to bring these pretty horses here at three o'clock?'

"That puts me jerry, 'n' I sure am sore when I thinks how he gets my goat.

"'Why, you big stiff!' I says. 'Ain't I been standin' here with these plugs fur a week? If you wants 'em, why don't you come 'n' tell me to lead 'em in? Do you think I'm a mind-reader?'

"His voice gets wild again.

"'Lead 'em in where?' he says. 'Through the lobby? Do you want to buy 'em tickets at the box-office? Will you have orchestra chairs for 'em or will front-row balcony do? Now beat it up that alley to the stage entrance, you doddering idiot!' he says. 'You've held up this rehearsal two hours!'

"Say, I've made some fierce breaks in my time, but that was the limit. It goes to show what a sucker anybody is at a new game. But at that, a child would have knowed those dogs didn't go in the front way.

"When I gets on to the stage with the hosses, there's guys 'n' dames standin' around all over it. The chicken comes 'n' shakes my mitt.

"'Say, kid,' she says, 'you'll hit the street for this sure. Where *have* you been?'

"Before I can tell her, here comes the pale guy down the aisle.

"'Everybody off stage!' he hollers. The bunch beats it to the sides. 'Now,' says the pale guy. 'We'll start the third act. Pixley,' he says to the chicken, 'I'll read your lines. You explain to Daniel Webster his cue, lines and business for your scene. Charlie, hold those horses.'

"The chicken starts to wise me up like he tells her. I'm a jock in the play, 'n' I has one line to say. 'He'll win, sir, never fear,' is the line. What another guy says to me before I says it she calls a cue, 'n' I learns that, too. I don't remember much what goes on that first day. I gets through my stunt O. K., except what I has to say - somehow, I can't get it off my chest louder'n a he-mouse can squeak.

"'If any one told me a horse would win, in that tone of voice,' says the pale guy to me, 'I'd go bet against him!' He keeps me sayin' it over 'n' over till pretty soon you can hear me nearly three feet away. 'That'll have to do for today,' says the pale guy. 'Everybody here at two o'clock to-morrow. I'll have the lobby swept out for your entrance, Daniel Webster,' he says to me.

"I tries the back door fur a change next day and they rehearse all afternoon. I'm here to say that pale guy is some dispenser of remarks. At plain 'n' fancy cussin' he's a bear.

"He's got the whole bunch buffaloed, except the chicken. She hands it back to him when it comes too strong.

"'Pixley,' he says to her once, 'your directions call for a quick exit. The audience will be able to stand it if you get off stage inside of ten minutes. Try and remember you are not stalling a Johnny with a fond farewell in this scene.'

"'That's a real cute crack,' says the chicken. 'But you've got your dates mixed. I can shoo a Johnny, even if he's in the profession,' she says, lookin' at him, 'quicker than a bum stage manager can fire a little chorus girl.'

"The pale guy's name is De Mott. He looks at her hard fur a minute, then he swallers the dose.

"'Proceed with the act,' he says.

"The show goes great the first night, far as I can see, but De Mott ain't satisfied.

"'It's dragging! It's dragging!' he keeps sayin' to everybody.

"A minute before I has to walk out on the stage, leadin' Edwin Booth, I can't think of nothin' but what I has to say. I gets one look at all them blurry faces, 'n' I goes into a trance.

"'More than life depends on this race!' I hears a voice say, about a mile off. That's my cue, but all I can remember is to tell him it's a cinch, 'n' say it loud.

"'The dog cops sure as hell!' I hollers.

"After the act De Mott rushes over tearin' at his collar like it's chokin' him.

"'Don't you even know the difference between a horse and a dog?' he yells at me.

"'If you sees this hound cough it up in the stretch often as I have, you calls him a dog yourself,' I says.

"I don't furget again after that, 'n' things go along smooth as silk from then on.

"The show runs along fur a week, but it don't make good.

"'The waving corn for this outfit!' says the chicken to me, Saturday night. 'The citizens of Peoria, Illinois, will have a chance to lamp my art before long.'

"She's got it doped right. We hit the road in jig-time. Banks makes a speech before we leaves.

"'Ladies and gentlemen,' he says, 'I thank you for your good work. Mr. De Mott will represent me on the road. I hope you will be a happy family, and I wish you success.'

"Outside of the chicken, I'm not stuck on the bunch. They're as cheap a gang as I'm ever up against. This De Mott guy is a cheese right, but he sure thinks he's the original bell-wether. He's strong fur the chicken, 'n' this makes the others sore at her. They don't have much to do with me neither, 'n' she don't fall fur De Mott, so her 'n' me sees each other a lot.

"She's a bug over hosses 'n' the track. She wants me to tell her all about trainin' a hoss 'n' startin' a hoss 'n' fifty other things besides.

"'I always lose,' she says. 'But then, I'm a rummy. Can you tell which horse is going to win, Blister?'

"'Sometimes,' I says.

"'When you go back to the track will you put me wise so I can win?' she says.

"'You bet I will, girlie!' I says. 'Any time I cut loose a good thing you gets the info right from the feed-box.'

"De Mott keeps noticin' us stickin' together. He's talkin' to her once when I'm passin' by.

"'He's on the square,' she says pretty loud. 'And that's more than you can say about a lot of people I know.'

"'That big ham was trying to knock you,' she says to me afterwards.

"We makes a bunch of towns. Nothin' very big - burgs like Erie 'n' Grand Rapids 'n' Dayton. Finally we hits St. Louis fur a two weeks' stand. This suits me. I'm sure tired of shippin' the dogs every few days.

"One night the chicken stops me as I'm takin' the pups to their kennel.

"'Come back for me, Blister,' she says, 'when you get your horses put up. There's a Johnny in this town that's pestering the life out of me. He wants me to go to 'Frisco with him.'

John Taintor Foote

"When I gets back to the theater I sees a green buzz-wagon at the stage door with a guy 'n' a shofe in it.

"The chicken has hold of my arm comin' out of the door, but she lets go of it 'n' then steps up straight to the buzz-wagon.

"'I can't keep my engagement with you this evening,' she says. 'My brother's in town and I'm going to be with him.'

"'Bring your brother along,' says the guy, 'n' I know by that he's got it bad.

"'I can't very well,' she says. 'We have some family matters to talk over. I'll see you some other evening.'

"The very next night a bunch of scenery tumbles over. The race is goin' on, 'n' Edwin Booth is layin' down to it right. A piece of scenery either falls under his feet or else jims the machine, I never knows which, anyhow, all of a sudden the hoss gets real footin'. Bingo! We're on our way like we're shot out of a gun. We go through all the scenery on that side 'n' Edwin Booth does a flop when he hits the brick wall at the end of the stage. The ole hound ain't even scratched. I ain't hurt neither.

"The curtain rings down 'n' De Mott comes a-lopin' to where I'm gettin' a painted grand-stand off of Edwin Booth's front legs.

"'In heaven's name what were you trying to do?' he says.

"'I was just practisin' one of them quick exits you're always talkin' about,' I says.

"'All right,' he says. 'Keep on practising till you come to that door! Follow on down the street till you reach the river and then jump in!'

"'I guess I'm fired - is that it?' I says.

"'You're a good guesser,' says De Mott.

"The chicken has come over by this time.

"'Are you hurt, Blister?' she says.

"'Not a bit, girlie,' I says, 'n' starts to go change my clothes.

"'Wait till I give you an order on the box-office for your money,' says De Mott.

"'Well, get busy,' I says to him. 'I've stood it around where you are about as long as is healthy.'

"'What's that?' says the chicken to De Mott. 'You don't mean to tell me you fired him!'

"'I don't mean to tell you *anything* that's none of your business,' says De Mott. 'Go dress for the next act!'

"'Not on your life!' she says. 'You can't fire him; it wasn't *his* fault! I'll write Banks a *lot* I know about you!'

"De Mott pulls out his watch.

"'I'll give you just *one minute* to start for your dressing-room,' he says to her.

"The chicken knocks the watch out of his hand.

"'*That* for your old turnip and you, too!' she says.

"'You're fired!' yells De Mott.

"'Oh, no, I ain't!' says the chicken. 'That's my way of breaking a contract and a watch at the same time. You needn't write an order for me,' she says. 'I'm overdrawn a week now.'

"When we're leavin', after we gets our street clothes on, De

John Taintor Foote

Mott stops us.

"'There's a way you can both get back,' he says to the chicken.

"'When I sell out,' says she, 'it'll be to a real man for real money, not to a cheap ham-fat for a forty-dollar job.'

"The chicken won't stay at the hotel where the bunch is that night, so we both moves over to another. When we pays our bill I have seven bucks left 'n' she has six.

"'We'll decide what to do in the morning, Blister,' she says. 'I've got a headache, so I think I'll hit the hay.'

"She goes to her room 'n' I sets 'n' studies how this is goin' to wind up, till three o'clock.

"We has breakfast together the next mawnin' about noon.

"'Well,' says the chicken, 'I've been up against it before, but this is tougher than usual. Everybody I know is broke or badly bent.'

"'Same here,' I says.

"'You poor kid!' she says. 'What'll you do?'

"'Don't worry none about me,' I says. 'I can get to New Awlins somehow - they're racin' down there. But what about you?'

"'If I could get back East,' she says, 'I know a floor-walker at Macy's who'll stake me to a job till I can get placed.'

"'You stick around here,' I says, when we're through eatin'. 'I'll go out 'n' give the burg a lookin' over.'

"'I've got that Johnny's phone number,' she says. 'I wonder if he'd stand for a touch without getting too fresh?'

"I goes to the desk 'n' wigwags the clerk. He's a fair-haired boy with a alabaster dome.

"'Are they runnin' poolrooms in the village?' I says.

"'Yes, sir,' he says. 'Pool and billiard room just across the street.'

"'Much obliged,' I says. I see the tomtit ain't got a man's size chirp in him, so I goes outside 'n' hunts up a bull.

"'Can you wise me up to a pony bazaar in this neck of the woods?' I says to him.

"'Go chase yourself,' he says. 'What do you think I am - a capper?'

"'Be a sport,' I says. 'Come through with the info - I ain't a live one. I'm a chalker, 'n' I'm flat. I'm lookin' fur a job.'

"He sizes me up fur quite a while.

"'Well,' he says at last, 'I guess if they trim you they'll earn it. Go down two blocks, then half a block to your right and take a squint at the saloon with the buffalo head over the bar.'

"I finds the saloon easy enough.

"'Make it a tall one,' I says to the barkeep.

"While I'm lappin' up the drink, a guy walks in 'n' goes through a door at the other end of the booze parlor.

"'Where does that door go to?' I says to the barkeep.

"'It's nothin' but an exit,' he says.

"'That's right in my line,' I says. 'I'll take a chance at it.'

John Taintor Foote

"When I opens the door I hears a telegraph machine goin'.

"'Just like mother used to make,' I says out loud, 'n' follows down a dark hall to the poolroom.

"I watches the New Awlins entries chalked up 'n' I sees a hoss called Tea Kettle in the third race. Now this Tea Kettle ain't a bad pup. He's owned by a couple of wise Ikes who never let him win till the odds are right. Eddie Murphy has this hoss 'n' Duckfoot Johnson's swipin' him.'

"'I wish I knew what they're doin' with that Tea Kettle to-day,' I says to myself, when I've looked 'em all over.

"I've been settin' there fur quite a while when a nigger comes in. I don't pay no attention to him at first, but I happen to see him fish a telegram out of his pocket 'n' look at it.

"'That ole nigger's got some dope,' I says to myself. 'I'll amble over 'n' try to kid it out of him.'

"I mosies over to where he's settin'. He puts the wire in his pocket when he sees me comin'. I sets down beside him 'n' goes to readin' the paper. Pretty soon I folds up the paper 'n' looks at the board.

"'That Tea Kettle might come through,' I says to the ole nigger.

"'Dat ain' likely,' he says. 'He ain' won fo' a coon's aige.'

"'I talks to his swipe not very long ago,' I says, ''n' he tells me he's good.'

"The ole nigger looks at me hard.

"'Whar does you hol' dis convahsation at?' he says.

"'Sheepshead,' I says.

"'Does you reccomember de name ob de swipe?' says the ole nigger.

"'Sure!' I says, 'I've knowed *him* all my life! His name is Duckfoot Johnson.'

"'Yes, suh!' he says. 'Yes, suh - an' what mought yo' name be?'

"'Blister Jones,' I says.

"'Why, man!' he says, 'I've heard ob you frequen'ly. Ma name am Johnson. Duckfoot is ma boy; hyars a tellegam fum him!'

"He pulls out the wire. 'T. K. in the third,' it says. I looks up at the board - Tea Kettle's twelve-to-one.

"I goes out of that poolroom on the jump 'n' runs all the way to the hotel. The chicken ain't in her room. I falls down-stairs 'n' looks all around - nothin' doin'. All of a sudden I sees her in the telephone booth.

"'Gimme that six bones quick!' I says when I've got the glass door open. She puts her hand over the phone.

"'Here, it's in my bag,' she says.

"I grabs the bag 'n' beats it. I gets the change out on my way back to the poolroom. The third race is still open, 'n' I gets ten bucks straight 'n' two to show on Tea Kettle. Then I goes over where ole man Johnson's settin'.

"'Whar does you go so quick like?' he says.

"'I'm after some coin,' I says, tryin' to ketch my breath. 'I've took a shot at the Tea Kettle hoss.'

"'I has bet on him,' he says, 'to ma fullest reso'ses.'

"'How much you got on?' I says.

"'Foh dollahs,' says ole man Johnson.

"Just then the telegraph begins to click.

"'They're off at New Orle-e-e-ns!' sings the operator. 'King Ja-a-ames first! Eldorado-o-o second! Anvil-l-l third!'

"The telegraph keeps a stutterin' 'n' a stutterin'.

"'Eldorado-o-o at the quarter a length! Anvil-l-l second a length! King Ja-a-ames third!' sings the operator.

"I looks at ole man Johnson. He looks at me.

"'Eldorado-o-o at the half by three lengths! Anvil-l-l second by two lengths! King Ja-a-ames third!' sings the operator.

"I looks at ole man Johnson. He don't look at me. He looks up at the ceilin' 'n' his lips is goin' like he's prayin'. Me? I'm wipin' the sweat off my face.

"'Eldorado-o-o in the stretch a half a length!' sings the operator. 'Anvil-l-l second a nose! Te-e-a Kettle third and coming fast!'

"If I gets a shock from that telegraph wire I don't jump any higher.

"'Howdy, howdy! *He's boilin now,*' yells ole man Johnson loud enough to bust your ear.

"Then that cussed telegraph stops right off.

"'Wire trouble at New Orleans,' says the operator.

"I sure hopes I never spends no more half-hours like I does then waitin' fur the New Awlins message. I thinks every minute ole man Johnson's goin' to croak if it don't come soon. In about ten years the telegraph begins to work again.

"'The result at New Orle-e-ens!' sings the operator. 'Te-e-ea Kettle wins by five lengths! Eldo -'

"But ole man Johnson lets out such a whoop I don't hear who finishes second 'n' third.

"I hustles up to the chicken's room when I'm back to the hotel. The transom's open when I gets to the door 'n' I hears a guy talkin'.

"'Don't misunderstand me,' he's savin'. 'You know perfectly the money's nothing to me, but why should I cut my own throat? If you'll go West instead of East, everything I have is yours!'

"'I don't misunderstand you,' says the chicken's voice. 'I have you sized up to a dot. I've met hundreds like *you*!'

"I knocks on the door.

"'Come,' says the chicken, 'n' I walks in. She's standin' with the table between her 'n' a swell-lookin' guy.

"'Mr. Chandler,' she says. 'Let me introduce you to my brother.'

"'How do you do?' says the swell guy. 'You have a charming sister.'

"'She's a great kid,' I says.

"'You don't look much alike,' says the swell guy.

"'She's not my full sister,' I says. 'Our mothers weren't the same.'

"The chicken coughs a couple of times.

"'That explains it,' says the swell guy.

"'Now,' I says to him, 'I hate to tie a can to one of sis's friend, but she's goin' East at six o'clock, 'n' she's got to pack her duds.'

"'Oh, Blister, *am* I?' says the chicken.

"'Yep, I hears from auntie,' I says, pullin' out the roll 'n' lay in' it on the table.

"The chicken gives a shriek, 'n' starts to hug me right in front of the swell guy.

"'I seem to be dee tro,' says he, 'n' backs out the door.

"'Where did you get the money?' says the chicken, countin' the roll. 'Why! There's *over a hundred here*!'

"I takes fifty bucks fur myself, 'n' hands her the rest.

"'I cops it at a poolroom,' I says. 'A ten-to-one shot comes through fur me. Now get busy. I'll send fur your trunk in ten minutes.'

"The chicken won't hear of ridin' in a street-car, so we takes a cab like a couple of Trust maggots.

"'I'll buy your ticket 'n' check your trunk fur you,' I says, when we get to the station. 'Where do you want to go? New York?'

"'Anywhere you say,' she says. . .

"I'm standin' there lookin' at her, lettin' this sink into my bean, 'n' she begins to get red.

"'Don't stand there gawking at me!' she says, stampin' her foot. 'Say something!'

"'How about this St. Louis guy?' I says. 'With all his -'

"'Oh, he was only a Johnny,' she says.

"'How about De Mott?' I says.

"'Ugh!' she says, makin' a face.

"I don't say nothin' after that till I has it all thought out. The start looks awful good, but I begins to weaken when I thinks of the finish.

"'You act just suffocated with pleasure,' says the chicken. But I don't pay no attention.

"'You'll be lucky if you gets a job swipin' fur your eats when you hit New Awlins,' I says to myself. 'Wouldn't you look immense with a doll on your staff?'

"'Now, listen,' I says to her, 'how long is this here panic goin' to last?'

"'You can search me,' she says.

"'Well, how long is this hundred goin' to last?' I says.

"'Not long,' she says.

"'That's the answer,' I says. 'Now, you hop a deep sea goin' rattler fur New York while the hoppin' 's good.'

"'But, Blister,' she says, 'at New Orleans you could win lots of money - think how much you've made already - and I could go to the races every day!'

"'Furget it,' I says. 'You think you're a wise girl. Why, you ain't nothin' but a child! A break like I has to-day don't come but seldom. If I cops the coin easy, like you figgers, why am I chambermaid to two dogs in a bum show at twenty-five per? Now slip me the price of a ticket to New York,' I says, 'or I goes 'n' buys it out of my own roll, 'n' then I ain't got enough left to get to New Awlins.'

"She don't say nothin' more, but hands me the dough. I buys her ticket 'n' checks her trunk fur her. She keeps real quiet till her rattler's ready. I kisses her good-by when they calls the train fur New York, 'n' still she don't say nothin'.

"'What's on your mind, girlie?' I says.

"'Nothing much,' she says. 'Only I'm letter perfect in the turnin'-down act, but when it's the other way - I ain't up in my lines.'" . . .

Blister waved to a waiter and I saw there was to be no more.

"Did you ever see her again?" I inquired.

"Now you're askin' questions," said Blister.

TRES JOLIE

The hot inky odors of a newspaper plant took me by the throat during my progress in the whiny elevator to the third floor.

Before attacking the day's editorial I tried to decide whether it was the nerve flicking clash of the linotypes, the pecking chatter of the typewriters, or the jarring rumble of the big cylinder presses that was taking the life out of my work. I was impartial in this, but gave it up.

And then a letter was dropped on the desk before me, and I recognized in the penciled address upon the envelope the unformed hand of Blister Jones.

"Dear Friend," the letter began, and somehow the ache behind my eyes died out as I read. 'I guess you are thinking me dead by this time on account of not hearing from me sooner in answer to yours. Well, this is to show you I am alive and kicking. I guess you have read how good the mare is doing. She is a good mare, as good as her dam. I had some mean luck with her at Nashville by her going lame for me, so she could not start in the big stake, but she is O. K. now. I note what you said about being sick. That is tough. Why don't you come to Louisville and see the mare run in the derby. If you would only bet, I can give you a steer that would put you right and pay all your expenses. Well, this is all for the present.

"Resp. "Blister Jones.

John Taintor Foote

"P. S. Now, be sure to come as I want you to see the mare. She is sure a good mare."

I laid the letter down with a sigh. The mare referred to was the now mighty Tres Jolie favorite for the Kentucky Derby. I had seen her once when a two-year-old, and I remembered Blister's pride as he told me she was to be placed in his hands by Judge Dillon.

Yes, I would be glad to see "the mare," and I longed for the free sunlit world of which she was a part, as for a tonic. But this was, of course, impossible. So long as hard undiscerning materialism demanded editorials - editorials I must furnish.

"Damn such a pen!" I said aloud, at its first scratch.

"Quite right!" boomed a deep voice. A big gentle hand fell on my shoulder and spun me away from the desk. "See here," the voice went on gruffly, "you're back too soon. We can't afford to take chances with *you*. Get out of this. The cashier'll fix you up. Don't let me see you around here again till - we have better pens," and he was gone before thanks were possible.

"I'm going to Churchill Downs to cover the derby for a Sunday special!" I sang to the sporting editor as I passed his door.

"The *Review of Reviews* might use it!" followed me down the hall, and I chuckled as I headed for the cashier's desk.

"Well, well, well!" was Blister's greeting. "Look who's here! I seen your ole specs shinin' in the sun clear down the line!"

I sniffed luxuriously.

"It smells just the same," I said. "Horses, leather and liniment! Where's Tres Jolie?"

"In the second stall," said Blister, pointing. "Wait a minute -

I'll have a swipe lead her out. Chick!" - this to a boy dozing on a rickety stool - "if your time ain't too much took up holdin' down that chair, this gentleman 'ud like to take a pike at the derby entry."

Like a polished red-bronze sword leaping from a black velvet scabbard the mare came out of her stall into the sunlight, the boy clinging wildly to the strap. She snorted, tossed her glorious head, and shot her hind feet straight for the sky.

"You, Jane, be a lady now!" yelled the boy, trying to stroke the arching neck.

"Why does he call her Jane?" I asked.

"Stable name," Blister explained. "Don't get too close - she's right on edge!" And after a pause, his eyes shining: "Can you beat her?"

I shook my head, speechless.

"Neither can *they*!" Blister's hand swept the two-mile circle of stalls that held somewhere within their big curve - the enemy.

The boy at the mare's head laughed joyously.

"They ain't got a chance!" he gloated.

"All right, Chick," said Blister. "Put her up! Hold on!" he corrected suddenly. "Here's the boss!" And I became aware of a throbbing motor behind me. So likewise did Tres Jolie.

"Whoa, Jane! Whoa, darling; it's mammy!" came in liquid tones from the motor.

The rearing thoroughbred descended to earth with slim inquiring ears thrown forward, and I remembered that Blister had described Mrs. Dillon's voice as "good to listen at."

John Taintor Foote

"Look, Virginia, she knows me!" the velvet voice exclaimed.

Another voice, rather heavy for a woman, but with a fascinating drawl in it, answered:

"Perhaps she fancies you have a milk bottle with you. Isn't this the one you and Uncle Jake raised on a bottle?"

"Yass'm, yass, Miss Vahginia, dat's her! Dat's ma Honey-bird!" came in excited tones from an ancient negro, who alighted stiffly from the motor and peered in our direction. As they approached, he held Mrs. Dillon by the sleeve, and I realized that for Uncle Jake the sun would never shine again.

Judge Dillon, a big-boned silent man, I had met. And after the shower of questions poured upon Blister had abated, and the mare had been gentled, petted and given a lump of sugar with a final hug, he presented me to his wife.

"My cousin, Miss Goodloe," said Mrs. Dillon, and I sensed a mass of tawny hair under the motor veil and looked into a pair of blue eyes set wide apart beneath a broad white brow. It was no time for details.

It developed that Miss Goodloe was from Tennessee, that she was visiting the Dillons at Thistle Ridge near Lexington, and that she liked a small book of verses of which I had been guilty. It further developed that Mrs. Dillon had talked me over with an aunt of mine in Cincinnati, that we were mutually devoted to Blister, and that he had described me to her as "the most educated guy allowed loose." This last I learned as Judge Dillon and Blister discussed the derby some distance from us.

"I feel awed and diffident in the presence of such learning," said Miss Goodloe almost sleepily. "Why did I neglect my opportunities at Dobbs Ferry!"

"I would give a good deal to observe you when you felt diffident, Virginia," said Mrs. Dillon, with a laugh like a silver bell. "Uncle Jake!" she called, "we are going now."

"I have heard of Uncle Jake," I said, as the old man felt his way toward us.

"Yes?" said Mrs. Dillon. "He insisted upon coming to *see* the derby." She dwelt ever so lightly upon the verb, and Uncle Jake caught it.

"No, Miss Sally," he explained, "dat ain' 'zackly what I mean. Hit's like dis - I just am boun' foh to hyah all de folks shout glory when ma Honey-bird comes home!"

"What if she ain't in front, Uncle Jake?" said Blister, helping the old man into the motor.

"Don't you trifle with me, boy!" replied Uncle Jake severely.

Derby day dawned as fair as turquoise sky and radiant sun could make it. I had slept badly. Until late the night before I had absorbed a haze of cigar smoke and the talk in the hotel lobby. Despite Blister's confidence I had become panicky as I listened. There had been so much assurance about several grave, soft-spoken horsemen who had felt that at the weight the favorite could not win.

"Nevah foh a moment, suh," one elderly well-preserved Kentuckian had said, "will I deny the Dillon mare the right to be the public's choice. But she has nevah met such a field of hosses as this, suh - and she lacks the bone to carry top weight against them."

There had been many nods of approval at this statement, and I had gone to the Dillon party for consolation. But when I reached their apartments I had found the judge more silent than ever, and Mrs. Dillon as nervous as myself. Only Miss Goodloe appeared as usual. Her drawl was soothingly indolent. She seemed entirely oblivious of any tenseness in the atmosphere, and I caught myself wondering what was behind those lazy-lidded blue eyes.

Back in the lobby once more I had found it worse than ever - so many were against the favorite. I had about decided that our hopes were doomed, when a call boy summoned me to the desk with the statement, "Gentleman to see you, sir."

There I had found Blister and I fairly hugged him as he explained that he had dropped in on the way to his "joint," as he called his hotel.

"Listenin' to the knockers?" he asked, reading me at once. "Furget it - them ole mint juleps is dead 'n' buried. You'll go dippy if you fall fur that stuff."

"But the weight!" I gasped.

"Say, they've got you goin' right, ain't they?" Blister exclaimed. "Now listen! *She can carry the grand-stand 'n' come home on the bit!* Get that fixed in your nut, 'n' then hit the hay."

"Thanks, I believe I shall," I said, and I had followed his advice, though it was long until sleep came to me.

But now as the blue-gray housetops of Louisville sparkled with tiny points of light, and the window-panes swam with pink-gold flame, I looked out over the still sleeping city and laughed aloud at my fears of the night before.

"A perfect day," I thought. "The favorite will surely win, and Blister and Uncle Jake and Mrs. Dillon will be made perfectly happy. A beautiful day, and a fitting one in which to fix the name of Tres Jolie among the equine stars!"

"We read some of your poetry last night after you had gone," said Mrs. Dillon, as we waited for the motor to take us to Churchill Downs. "I liked it, and I don't care for verse as a rule, except Omar. I dote on *The Rubaiyat;* don't you?"

"Yes, indeed," I replied. "I can't quite swallow his philosophy, but he puts it all so charmingly. Some of his pictures are most alluring."

"Do learned persons ever long for the *wilderness*, and the *bough*, and - the other things?" Miss Goodloe asked innocently.

"Quite frequently," I assured her.

She affected a sigh of relief.

"That's such a help," she said. "It makes them seem more like the rest of us."

A huge motor-car wheeled from the line at the curb and glided past us. A man in the tonneau lifted his hat high above his head as he saw Judge Dillon.

"Oh, you Tres Jolie!" he called with a smile. "The best luck in the world to you, Judge!" It was an excessively rich New Yorker, who owned one of the horses about to run in the derby.

"Oh, you Rob Roy!" called back Judge Dillon, also raising his hat. "The same to you, Henry!" And suddenly there was a tug at my nerves, for I realized that this was the *salut de combat*.

But Uncle Jake, his faith in his "Honey-bird" unshaken as the time drew near, rode in placid contentment on the front seat as we sped to the track. We passed, or were passed by, many motor-cars from which came joyous good wishes as the Dillons were recognized. Each packed and groaning street-car held some one who knew our party, and "Oh, you Tres Jolie!" they howled as we swept by. The old negro's ears drank all this in. It was as wine to his spirit. He hummed a soft minor accompaniment to the purring motor, and leaning forward I caught these words:

John Taintor Foote

"Curry a mule an' curry a hoss,
Keep down trubbul wid de stable boss!"

"Luck to her, Judge!" called the man at the gates, as he waved us through. "Ah've bet my clothes on her!"

"You'll need a barrel to get home in!" yelled a voice from a buggy. "The Rob Roy hoss'll beat her and make her like it!"

"You-all are from the East, Ah reckon," we heard the gateman reply. "Ah've just got twenty left that says we raise 'em gamer in Kentucky than up your way!"

At the stables we found Blister.

"How is she?" asked Judge Dillon.

"She's ready," was the answer. "It's all over, but hangin' the posies on her."

"Lemme feel dis mayah," said Uncle Jake, and Mrs. Dillon guided him into the stall.

"I'd like to give her one little nip before she goes to the post, Judge," I heard Blister say in a low voice.

"Not a drop," came the quick reply. "If she can't win on her own courage, she'll have to lose."

"Judge Dillon won't stand fur hop - he won't even let you slip a slug of booze into a hoss," Blister had once told me. I had not altogether understood this at the time, but now I looked at the big quiet man with his splendid sportsmanship, and loved him for it.

A roar came from the grand-stand across the center-field.

"They're off in the first race," said Blister. "Put the saddle on her, boys;" and when this was accomplished: "Bring her out -

it's time to warm up."

I had witnessed Tres Jolie come forth once before and I drew well back, but it was Mrs. Dillon who led the thoroughbred from the stall. She was breathing wonderful words. Her voice was like the cooing of a dove. Tres Jolie appeared to listen.

"She don't handle like that fur us, does she, Chick?" said Blister.

"Nope," said the boy addressed. "I guess she's hypnotized."

"How do you do it?" I inquired of Mrs. Dillon as she led the mare to the track, the rest of us following.

"She's my precious lamb, and I'm her own mammy," was the lucid explanation.

"Now you know," said Blister to me. "Pete!" he called to a boy, approaching, "I want this mare galloped a slow mile. Breeze her the last eighth. Don't take hold of her any harder'n you have to. Try 'n' *talk* her back."

"I got you," said the boy, as Blister threw him up. Mrs. Dillon let go of the bridle. Tres Jolie stood straight on her hind legs, made three tremendous bounds, and was gone. We could see the boy fighting to get her under control, as she sped like a bullet down the track.

"I guess Pete ain't usin' the right langwige," said the boy called Chick, with a wide grin.

"Maybe she ain't listenin' good," added another boy.

"Cut out the joshin' 'n' get her blankets ready," said Blister with a frown.

"I think we'd better start," suggested Judge Dillon.

John Taintor Foote

"Aren't you terribly excited?" I asked Miss Goodloe curiously, as she walked cool and composed by my side. My own heart was pounding.

"Of course," she drawled.

"This girl is made of stone," I thought.

The band was playing *Dixie* as we climbed the steps of the grand-stand, and the thousands cheered until it was repeated. Hands were thrust at the Dillons from every side, and until we found our box, continued shouts of, "Oh, you Tres Jolie!" rose above the crash of the band.

I had witnessed many races in the past and been a part of many racing crowds but never one like this. These people were Kentuckians. The thoroughbred was part of their lives and their traditions. Through him many made their bread. Over the fairest of all their fair acres he ran, and save for their wives and children they loved him best of all.

Once each year for many years they had come from all parts of the smiling bluegrass country to watch this struggle between the satin-coated lords of speed that determined which was king. This journey was like a pilgrimage, and worship was in their shining eyes, as tier on tier I scanned their eager faces.

And now three things happened. A bugle called, and called again. The crowd grew deathly still. And Mrs. Dillon, in a voice that reminded me of a frightened child, asked:

"Where is Blister?"

"He'll be here," said Judge Dillon, patting her hand. And even as a megaphone bellowed: "*We are now ready for the thirty-ninth renewal of the Kentucky Derby!*" Blister squeezed through the crowd to the door of the box.

He was a rock upon which we immediately leaned.

"Everything all right?" I asked.

"Fine as silk," he said cheerfully, dropping into a seat. "You'll see a race hoss run to-day! Here they come! She's in front!" And held to a proud sedateness by their tiny riders, the contenders in the derby filed through the paddock-gate.

At the head of these leashed falcons was a haughty, burnished, slender-legged beauty - the proudest of them all. Her neck was curving to the bit and she seemed to acknowledge with a gracious bow the roar of acclamation that greeted her. She bore the number 1 upon her satin side, and dropping my eyes to my program I read:

1. Tres Jolie - b. m. by Hamilton - dam Alberta. John C. Dillon, Lexington, Kentucky. (Manders - blue and gold.)

"What sort of jockey is Manders?" I asked Blister.

"Good heady boy," was the reply.

"Virginia, oh, Virginia, isn't she a lamb?" gasped Mrs. Dillon.

"She's a stuck-up miss," said Miss Goodloe in an even tone, and I almost hated her.

Number 2 I failed to see as they paraded past.

Number 3 was a gorgeous black, with eyes of fire, powerful in neck and shoulders, and with a long driving hip. He was handsome as the devil and awe-inspiring. Applause from the stands likewise greeted him, though it was feeble to the howl that had met the favorite.

"There's the one we've got to beat," Blister stated.

"Good horse," said Judge Dillon quietly.

3. Rob Roy - bl. s. by Tempus Fugit - dam Marigold. Henry

L. Whitley, New York City. (Dawson - green and white.)

I read. I followed him with my eyes and wished him some-where else. He looked so overpowering - he and the millions behind him. . . .

At last, a quarter of a mile away, they halted in a gorgeous shifting group. And the taut elastic webbing of the barrier that was to hold them from their flight a little longer, was stretched before them.

They surged against it like a parti-colored wave, and then receding, surged again, but always the narrow webbing held them back. I found the blue and gold. It was almost without motion - it did not shift and whirl with the rest.

"Ain't she the grand actor?" said Blister with delight. "The best mannered thing at the barrier ever I saw."

Then for a moment I lost the colors that had held my gaze. They were blotted out and crowded back by other colors. In that instant the wave conquered. It grew larger and larger. It was coming like the wind. But where was the blue and gold?

I was answered by a heaven-cleaving shout that changed in the same breath to a despairing groan. It was as though a giant had been stricken deep while roaring forth his battle-cry. The thousands had seen what I had missed - their hopes in an instant were gone. In the stillness that followed, a harsh whisper reached me.

"*She's left! She's left!*" Then an uncanny laugh. The rock had broken.

The wave was greeted by silence. A red bay thundered in the lead. Then came a demon, hard held, with open mouth, and number 3 shone from his raven side. Followed a flying squadron all packed together, their hoofs rolling like drums. And then came aching lengths, and my eyes filled with tears and something gripped my heart and squeezed it as Tres Jolie, skimming like an eager swallow, fled past undaunted by that hopeless gap.

"Whar my baby at?" asked Uncle Jake. He had heard the groan and the silence, and fear was in his voice.

"Oh - Uncle Jake -" began Mrs. Dillon. "They -" her voice broke.

"Dey ain' left her at de post? Doan' tell me dat, Miss Sally!"

Mrs. Dillon nodded as though to eyes that saw. Uncle Jake seemed to feel it.

"How fah back? How fah back?" he demanded.

"She ain't got a chance, Uncle Jake!" said Blister, and dropped his head on his arm lying along the railing.

"How fah back?" insisted the old negro.

Blister raised his head and gazed.

"Twenty len'ths," he said, and dropped it again.

"Doan' you fret, Miss Sally," Uncle Jake encouraged. "She'll beat 'em yet!"

"Not this time, old man," said Judge Dillon very gently. He was tearing his program carefully into little pieces, with big shaking hands. . . .

The horses were around the first turn, and the battle up the back stretch had begun. The red bay was still leading.

"Mandarin in front!" said some one behind us. "Rob Roy second and running easy - the rest nowhere!"

John Taintor Foote

"Jes' you wait!" called Uncle Jake.

"You ole fool nigger!" came Blister's muffled voice.

Even at that distance I could have told which one was last. The same effortless floating stride I had noticed long ago was hers as Tres Jolie, foot by foot, ate up the gap. At the far turn she caught the stragglers and one by one she cut them down.

"Oh, gallant spirit!" I thought. "If they had given you but half a chance!"

I lost her among a melee of horses, on the turn, as the leader swung into the stretch. It was the same red bay, but now the boy on the black horse moved his hands forward a little and his mount came easily to the leader's side. There was a short struggle between them and the bay fell back.

"Mandarin's done!" cried the voice behind us. "Rob Roy on the bit!"

"I might have known it!" I thought bitterly. "He looked it all along."

Then a gentle buzzing sprang up like a breeze. It was a whisper that grew to a muttering, and then became a rumble and at last one delirious roar. The giant had recovered, and his mighty cry brought me to my feet, my heart in my throat - for "*Tres Jolie*" he roared . . . and coming! . . . coming!! . . . coming!!! . . . I saw the blue and gold!

A maniac rose among us and flung his fists above his head. He called upon his gods - and then that magic name - "*Tres Jolie*," he shrieked: "*Oh, Baby Doll!*" It was Blister - and I marveled.

I had seen him stand and lose his all without a sign of feeling. But now he raved and cursed and prayed and plead with his "Girlie!" - his "Baby Doll!", and with the last atom of her strength his sweetheart answered the call.

She reached, heaven alone knows how, the flank of the flying black, and inch by inch she crept along that flank until they struggled head to head.

"Oh, you black dog!" howled Blister, wild triumph in his voice. "You've got to beat a race hoss *now*!"

As though he heard, the black horse flattened to his work. Almost to the end he held her there, eye meeting eye. The task was just beyond him. Even as they shot under the wire, he faltered. But it was very close, and the shrieking hysterical grand-stand grew still and waited.

I glanced at Blister. He was leaning forward, almost crouching, his face ashen, his eyes on the number board.

Then slowly the numbers swung into view, and "*1, 3, 7,*" I read.

There was a roar like the falling of ten thousand forest trees. These words flashed through my mind. "We'll know about *her* when she goes the route, carryin' weight against class." . . . . Yes, we knew about *her* - now!

I saw Mrs. Dillon's lips move at Uncle Jake's ear. He raised his sightless eyes to the sky, his head nodding. It was as though he visioned paradise and found it good indeed.

I saw Blister's face turn from gray to red, from red to purple. The tenseness went out of his body, and suddenly he was gone, fighting his way through the crowd toward the steps.

I saw Judge Dillon's big arm gather in his trembling wife, and he held her close while the heavens rocked.

These things I saw through a blur, and then I felt Miss Goodloe sway at my side. She clutched at the railing, missed it and sank slowly into her seat. I but glimpsed a white face in which the eyes had changed from blue to violet, when it was

John Taintor Foote

covered by two slender gloved hands.

"Are you ill?" I called, as I bent above her.

She shook her head.

"It was too much," I barely heard.

I stood bewildered, and then my stupid mind cast out a soulless image that it held and fixed the true one there.

"I rarely make this kind of a fool of myself," she said at last.

"That I can quite believe," I replied, smiling down at her. She returned the smile with one that held a fine good comradeship, and we seemed to have known each other long. . . .

A crowd had packed themselves before the stall. As we reached it Blister appeared in the doorway.

"Get back! Get back!" he ordered, and pointing to the panting mare: "Don't you think she's earned a right to breath?"

The crowd fell away, except one rather shabby little old man.

"No one living," said he, "appreciates what she has done moh than myself, suh, but I desiah to lay ma hand on a real race mayah once moh befoh I die!"

Blister's face softened.

"Come on in, Mr. Sanford," he invited. "Why *you* win the derby once, didn't you?"

"Thank you, suh. Yes, suh, many yeahs ago," said the little old man, and removing his battered hat he entered the stall, his white head bare.

Mrs. Dillon's face as she, too, entered the stall was tear-wet and alight with a great tenderness.

A boy dodged his way to where we stood. His face and the front of his blue and gold jacket were encrusted with dirt.

"You shoe-maker!" was Blister's scornful greeting.

"Honest to Gawd it wasn't my fault, Judge," the boy piped, sniffling. "Honest to Gawd it wasn't! That sour-headed bay stud of Henderson's swung his ugly butt under the mare's nose, 'n' just as I'm takin' back so the dog won't kick a leg off her, that mutt of a starter lets 'em go!"

"All right, sonny," said the judge. "You rode a nice race when you did get away."

"Much obliged, sir. I just wanted to tell you," said the boy, and he disappeared in the crowd as Judge Dillon joined those in the stall.

I stayed outside watching the group about Tres Jolie, and never had my heart gone out to people more. Deeply I wished to keep them in my life. . . I wondered if we would ever meet again. But pshaw! - I was nothing to them. Well, I would go back to Cincinnati when they left in the morning. . . .

"Can't we have you for a week at Thistle Ridge?" Mrs. Dillon stood looking up at me.

"Why, that's very kind - " I stammered.

"The north pasture is a *wilderness* this year, the *loaf of bread, the jug of wine* and the *bough* are waiting. You can, of course, furnish your own *verses*."

"The picture is almost perfect," I said, and glanced at Miss Goodloe.

"Virginia, dear -" prompted Mrs. Dillon.

John Taintor Foote

"As a *thou* - I always strive to please," drawled that blue-eyed young person. Oh, that I had been warned by her words!

Our purring flight to Louisville, when the day was done, became a triumph that mocked the dead Caesars. Of this the old negro on the front seat missed little. He was singing, softly singing. And leaning forward I listened.

"Curry a mule an' curry a hoss,
Keep down trubbul wid de stable boss!"

sang Uncle Jake.

OLE MAN SANFORD

"Do you happen to notice a old duck that comes to the stalls at Loueyville just after the derby?" asked Blister.

"Was his name Sanford, and did he wish to pat the mare?" I asked in turn.

"That's him," said Blister. "Ole man Sanford. It ain't likely you ever heard of him, but everybody on the track knows him, if they ever hit the Loueyville meetin'. They never charge him nothin' to get into the gates. He ain't a owner no more, but way back there before I'm alive he wins the Kentucky Derby with Sweet Alice, 'n' from what I hears she was a grand mare. Ole man Sanford breeds Sweet Alice hisself. In them days he's got a big place not far from Loueyville. They tell me his folks get the land original from the govament, when it's nothin' but timber. I hears once, but it don't hardly sound reasonable, that they hands over a half a million acres to the first ole man Sanford, who was a grandaddy of this ole man Sanford. If that's so, Uncle Sam was more of a sport in them days than since.

"I don't know how they pry it all loose from him, but one mawnin' ole man Sanford wakes up clean as a whistle. They've copped the whole works - he ain't got nothin'. So he goes to keepin' books fur a whisky house in Loueyville, 'n' he holds the job down steady fur twenty years. The only time he quits pen-pushin' is when they race at Churchill Downs. From the first minute the meetin' opens till get-away day comes he's

John Taintor Foote

bright eyes at the rat hole. He don't add up no figgers fur nobody then. He just putters around the track. He's doped out as sort-a harmless by the bunch.

"After the Tres Jolie mare wins the derby fur me, ole man Sanford makes my stalls his hang-out. I ain't kickin', all he wants to do is to look at the mare 'n' chew the rag about her. That satisfies him completely.

"'Of all the hosses, suh, who have been a glory to our state,' he says, 'but one otheh had as game a heart as this superb creature. I refer to Sweet Alice, suh - a race mayah of such quality that the world marveled. Not in a boastful manner, suh, but with propah humility, let me say that I had the honor to breed and raise Sweet Alice, and that she bore my colors when she won the tenth renewal of our great classic.'

"He tells this to everybody that comes past the stalls, 'n' it ain't long till he begins to bring people around to look the mare over. From that he gets to watchin' how the swipes take care of her. Pretty soon he begins to call 'em if things ain't done to suit him.

"'Boy,' he'll say, 'that bandage is tighter than I like to see it. Always allow the tendon a little play - do not impaieh the suhculation.'

"The boys eat this stuff up - it tickles 'em. They treat him respectful 'n' do what he tells 'em.

"'Everything O. K. to-day, sir?' they'll say.

"Ole man Sanford don't tumble they're kiddin' him.

"'Ah have nothing to complain of,' he says.

"It ain't long till he's overseein' my whole string of hosses, just like he owns 'em. Man, he sure does enjoy hisself! He won't trade places with August Belmont.

"I'm gettin' Trampfast ready fur a nice little killin'. He's finished away back in two starts, but he runs both races without a pill. This hoss is a dope. He's been on it fur two seasons. He won't beat nothin' without his hop. But when he gets just the right mixture under his hide he figgers he can beat any kind of a hoss, 'n' he's about right at that. He furgets all about his weak heart with the nutty stuff in him. He thinks he's a ragin' lion. He can't wait to go out there 'n' eat up them kittens that's goin' to start against him.

"One mawnin' my boy Pete takes the Trampfast hoss out fur a trial.

"'If he'll go six furlongs in about fourteen,' I says to Pete, 'he's right. If he tries to loaf on you, shake him up; but if he's doin' his work nice, let him suit hisself 'n' keep the bat off him. I want to see what he'll do on his own.'

"'I think he'll perform to-day,' says Pete. 'He's felt real good to me fur the last week.'

"Ole man Sanford's standin' there listenin'. When the work-out starts he ketches the time with a big gold stop-clock that he fishes out of his shiny ole vest. The clock's old, too - it winds with a key - but at that she's a peach!

"'That's a fine clock,' I says to him. He don't take his eyes off the hoss comin' round the bend.

"'He's running with freedom and well within himself,' he says. 'That quatah was in twenty-foh flat! Yes, suh, this watch was presented to me by membahs of the Breedah's Association to commemorate the victory of Sweet Alice in the tenth renewal of our classic. You have heard me speak of Sweet Alice?'

"'Yes, you told me about her, Mr. Sanford,' I says. 'That's sure some clock.'

"'If he does not faltah in the stretch, suh,' says ole man

John Taintor Foote

Sanford, 'I will presently show you the one minute and fohteen seconds you desiah upon its face.'

"The ole man's a good judge of pace, - Trampfast comes home bang in the fourteen notch.

"When Pete gets down at the stalls, ole man Sanford walks up to him.

"'Hyah is a dollah foh you, boy,' he says, 'n' hands Pete a buck. 'That was a well-rated trial.'

"Pete looks at the silver buck 'n' then at ole man Sanford 'n' then at me.

"'What the hell -' he says.

"'You rough neck!' I says to Pete. Don't you know how to act when a gentleman slips you somethin'?'

"'But look a-here,' says Pete. 'He ain't got -' I gives Pete a poke in the slats. 'Much obliged, sir,' he says, 'n' puts the bone in his pocket.

"'You are entirely welcome, mah boy,' says ole man Sanford, wavin' his hand.

"'Say,' Pete says to me, 'I think this hoss'll cop without shot in the arm. He's awful good!'

"'Not fur mine,' I says. 'He can run fur Sweeney when he ain't got no hop in him. Just let some sassy hoss look him in the eye fur two jumps 'n' he'll holler, "Please, mister, don't!" Yea, bo',' I says, 'I know this pup too well. When he's carryin' my kale he'll be shoutin' hallelooyah with a big joy pill under his belt.'

"I furgets all about ole man Sanford bein' there. You don't talk about hoppin' one with strangers listening but he's around so much I never thinks. All of a sudden he's standin' in front of me lookin' like there's somethin' hurtin' him.

"'What's the matter, Mr. Sanford?' I says.

"'I gathah from yoh convahsation,' says he, 'that it is yoh practise to supplement the fine courage that God has given the thoroughbred with vile stimulants. Am I correct in this supposition, suh?'

"'Why, yes -' I says, kind-a took back. 'When they need it I sure gives it to 'em.'

"Ole man Sanford draws hisself up 'n' looks at me like I'm a toad.

"'Suh,' he says, 'the man who does that degrades himself and the helpless creature that Providence has placed in his keeping! Not only that, suh, but he insults the name of the thorough-bred and all it stands for, still tendahly cherished by some of us. Ah have heard of this abhorant practise that has come as a part of this mercenary age, and, suh, Ah abominate both it and the man who would be guilty of such an act!'

"'Why, look-a here, Mr. Sanford,' I says. 'They're all doin' it. If you're goin' to train hosses you've got to get in the band wagon. If *you* can't give the owner a run fur his money he'll find somebody to train 'em who can!'

"'Do you mean to tell me, suh, the wonderful courage displayed by that mayah when the time came, was false?' says ole man Sanford, pointin' at Tres Jolie's stall. 'Ah saw strong men, the backbone of this state, suh,' he says, 'watch that mayah come home with tears in their eyes. Were their natures moved to the depths by an insulting counterfeit of greatness?'

"'Why, sure not!' I says. 'But all hosses ain't like this mare.'

"'They are not, suh!' says ole man Sanford. 'Noh were they intended to be! But few of us are ordained foh the heights.

John Taintor Foote

However,' he says, puttin' his hand on my shoulder, 'Ah should not censure you too strongly, young man. In fohcing yoh hawsses to simulate qualities they do not possess, you are only a part of yoh times. This is the day of imitation - I find it between the covahs of yoh books - I hear it in the music yoh applaud - I see it riding by in motah-cars. Imitation - all imitation!'

"I ain't hep to this line of chatter - it's by me. But I dopes it out he's sore at automobiles,

"'What's wrong with 'em?' I says to him.

"'Ah don't feel qualified to answer yoh question, suh,' he says. 'Ah believe the blind pursuit and worship of riches is almost entirely responsible. It has bred a shallowness and superficiality in and towahds the finah things of life. But the historian will answer yoh question at a later day. He can bring a calmness to the task which is impossible to one surrounded and bewildered by it all.'

"I ain't any wiser'n I was, but I don't say nothin'. The old man acts like he's studyin' about somethin'.

"'Who owns the hawss that just trialed three-quahtahs in fohteen?' he says, after while.

"'Jim Sigsbee up at Cynthiana,' I says.

"'Is Mr. Sigsbee awaheh of the - method you pursue with regahd to falsely stimulating his hawss?' says ole man Sanford.

"'Well, I guess yes!' I says. 'Jim won't bet a dollar on him unless he's got the hop in him.'

"'Ah shall write to him,' says ole man Sanford, 'n' beats it down the track toward the gates.

"I don't see him fur over a week. I figger he's sore at me fur dopin' hosses. It's a funny thing but, I'm a son-of-a-gun if I don't miss the ole duck. From the way they talk I see the boys kind-a miss him, too.

"'I wonder where ole Pierpont's at?' I hears Chick say to Skinny. 'Gone East to see one of his hosses prepped fur the Brooklyn, I guess.'

"'Naw,' says Skinny; 'you got that wrong. He's goin' to send a stable to Urope, 'n' Todd Sloan's tryin' to get a contrac' from him as exercise-boy. Ole Pierpont's watchin' Todd work out a few so he kin size up his style.'

"I've wrote Jim Sigsbee Trampfast's ready, but I don't enter the hoss 'cause I know Jim wants to come over 'n' bet a piece of money on him. I don't hear from Jim, 'n' I wonder why.

"One day I'm settin' in front of the stalls 'n' here comes ole man Sanford down the line.

"'Why, hello, Mr. Sanford!' I says. 'We sort-a figgered you'd quit us. Things ain't gone right since you left. The boys need you to keep 'em on their toes.'

"'Ah have not deserted you intentionally, suh,' he says. 'Since Ah saw you last an old friend of mine has passed to his rewahd. The Hono'able James Tullfohd Fawcett is no moh, suh - a gallant gentleman has left us.'

"'That's too bad,' I says. 'Did he leave a family?'

"'He did not, suh,' says ole man Sanford. 'Ah fell heir to his entiah estate, only excepting the silvah mug presented to his beloved mothah at his birth by Andrew Jackson himself, suh. This he bequeathed to the public, and it will soon be displayed at the rooms of the Historical Society named in his last will and testament.'

"'Did you get much out of it?" I says.

"'He had already endowed me with a friendship beyond price, suh,' he says. 'His estate was not a large one as such things go - some twelve hundred dollahs, I believe.'

"'That's better'n breakin' a leg,' I says.

"'You will, perhaps, be interested to learn,' he says, 'that Ah have pu'chased the hawss Trampfast with a po'tion of the money. Hyah is a lettah foh you from Mr. Sigsbee relative to the mattah.' He hands me a letter, but I can't hardly read it - his buyin' this hop-head gets my goat.

"'What you goin' to do with him?' I says. 'Race him?'

"'That is ma intention, suh,' he says. 'Ah expect to keep him in yoh hands. But, of co'se, suh, the hawss will race on his merits and without any sawt of stimulant.'

"I ain't stuck on the proposition. The Trampfast hoss can't beat a cook stove without the hop. I hate to see the ole man burn up his dough on a dead one.

"'Now, Mr. Sanford,' I says, 'times has changed since you raced. If you'll let me handle this hoss to suit myself I think I can make a piece of money fur you. The game ain't like it was once, 'n' if you try to pull the stuff that got by thirty years ago, they'll trim you right down to the suspenders. They ain't nothin' crooked about slippin' the hop into a hoss that needs it.'

"'As neahly as I can follow yoh fohm of speech,' says ole man Sanford, 'you intend to convey the impression that the practise of stimulating a hawss has become entirely propah. Am I correct, suh?'

"'That's it,' I says. ''N' you can gamble I'm right.'

"'Is the practise allowed under present day racing rules?' says ole man Sanford, 'n' I think I've got him goin'.

"'Why, sure not,' I says. 'But how long would a guy last if he never broke a racin' rule?'

"'Out of yoh own mouth is yoh augument condemned, suh,' says ole man Sanford. 'Even in this day and generation the rules fohbid it - and let me say, suh, that should a trainah, a jockey, or any one connected with a stable of mine, be guilty of wilfully violating a racing rule, Ah would discharge him at once, suh!'

"'*You goin' to race on the level all the time?*' I says.

"'If by that expression you mean hono'ably and as a gentleman - yes, suh!'

"'*Good night, nurse!*' I says. 'You'll go broke quick at that game!'

"'Allow me to remind you that that is ma own affaih, suh,' says ole man Sanford, 'n' the argument's over. His ideas date back so far they're mildewed, but I see I can't change 'em. He don't belong around a race track no more'n your grandmother!

"'All right, Mr. Sanford!' I says. 'You're the doctor! We'll handle him just like you say.'

"Peewee Simpson has come over to chew the rag with me, 'n' he hears most of this talk.

"'Wait till I call the boys,' he says, when ole man Sanford goes in to look at the hoss.

"'What fur?' I says.

"'Family prayers,' says Peewee.

"I throws a scraper at him, 'n' he goes on down the line singin', *Onward, Christian Soldiers.*

John Taintor Foote

"Ole man Sanford orders a set of silks. He's got to send away fur the kind he wants 'n' he won't let me start his hoss till they come. Nobody but big stables pays attention to colors, so I tries to talk him out of the notion, - nothin' doin'!

"'Ma colors were known and respected in days gone by, suh,' he says. 'Ah owe it to the public who reposed confidence in the puhple and white, to fly ma old flag when Ah once moh take the field. Yes, suh.'

"'Purple 'n' white!' I says. 'Them's the colors of the McVay stable!'

"'Ah was breeding stake hawsses, suh,' says ole man Sanford, 'when his mothah's milk was not yet dry upon the lips of young McVay.'

"When the silks come, I picks out a real soft spot for Trampfast. It's a six furlong ramble fur has-beens 'n' there's sure a bunch of kioodles in it! Most of 'em ought to be on crutches. My hoss has showed me the distance in fourteen, 'n' that's about where this gang'll stagger home. With the hop in him the Trampfast hoss'll give me two seconds better. He ought to be a swell bet. But the hop puts all the heart in him there is - he ain't got one of his own. If he runs empty he'll lay down sure. I can't hop him, so I won't bet on him with counterfeit money.

"The mawnin' of the race ole man Sanford's at the stalls bright 'n' early. He's chipper as a canary. He watches Chick hand-rub the hoss fur a while 'n' then he pulls out a roll 'n' eases Chick two bucks. I pipes off the roll. The ole man sees me lookin' at it.

"'Ah intend to wageh moderately today,' he says. 'And Ah have brought a small sum with me foh the puhpose.'

"'What you goin' to bet on?' I says.

"'Ma own hawss, of co'se, suh,' he says. 'It is ma custom to back only ma own hawsses or those of ma friends.'

"I don't say nothin'. I'm wise by this time, he plays the game to suit hisself, but it sure makes me sick. I hate as bad to see the ole man lose his dough as if it's mine.

"I goes over 'n' sets down on the track fence.

"'When you train a hoss fur a guy you do like he says, don't you?' I says to myself. 'You don't own this hoss, 'n' the owner don't want him hopped. They ain't but one answer - don't hop him.'

"'But look-a here,' I says back to myself. 'If you sees a child in wrong, you tells him to beat it, don't you? It ain't your child, is it? Well, this ole man ain't nothin' but a child. If he was, he'd let you hop the hoss, 'n' make a killin' fur him.' I argues with myself this way, but they can't neither one of us figger it out to suit the other.

"'I wish the damned ole fool had somebody else a-trainin' his dog!' I thinks after I've set there a hour 'n' ain't no further along 'n I was when I starts.

"When it's gettin' towards post time, ole man Sanford hikes fur the stand.

"'Skinny,' I says, 'amble over to the bettin' shed 'n' watch what the ole man does. As soon as he's got his kale down, beat it back here on the jump, 'n' tell me how much he gets on 'n' what the odds are.'

"In about ten minutes here comes Skinny at a forty shot.

"'He bets a hundred straight at fifteen-to-one! What do you know about that?' he hollers.

"'That settles it!' I says. 'Chick, get them two bottles that's hid

John Taintor Foote

under the rub-rags in the trunk! Now, ole Holler-enough,' I says to the Tramp, 'you may be a imitation hoss, but we're goin' to make you look so much like the real thing your own mother won't know you! . . .'

"When Trampfast starts fur the paddock, his eyes has begun to roll 'n' he's walkin' proud.

"'He thinks he's the Zar of Rushy,' says Chick. 'He'll be seein' pink elephants in a minute.'

"I don't find ole man Sanford till they're at the post. He's standin' by the fence at the wire.

"The start's bein' held up by the Tramp. He's sure puttin' on a show - the hop's got him as wild as a eagle. It's too far away fur the ole man to see good, so I don't put him hep it's his hoss that's cuttin' the didoes.

"Just then Chick comes up.

"'I hear you get a nice bet down on your hoss, Mr. Sanford,' he says. 'I sure hope he cops.'

"'Thank you, ma boy,' says ole man Sanford. 'I only placed a small wageh, but at vehy liberal odds. Ah shall profit materially should he win his race.'

"'If he gets away good he'll roll,' says Chick. 'There's no class to that bunch, 'n' he's a bear with a shot in him. But he's a bad actor when he's hopped - look at the fancy stuff he's pullin' now!'

"'You are mistaken, ma boy,' says ole man Sanford. 'This hawss has had no stimulant *to-day*.'

"Like a nut I've furgot to tell the boys the ole man ain't on. I tries to give Chick the high sign, but he's watchin' the hosses, 'n' before I can get to him he belches up the glad news.

"'If *he* ain't hopped one never was!' he says. 'We put a fierce shot in him. Look at him act if you don -'

"I kick his shin off right there, but it's too late, ole man Sanford gets pale as a rag.

"'How dare you -' he says, 'n' stops. 'But Ah shall prevent it!' he says, 'n' starts fur the judge's stand. He ain't got a chance - just then they get away, 'n' he turns back to me when he hears the crowd holler, 'They're off!'

"'Young man,' he says, pointin' at me, 'n' he's shakin' like he's cold. 'What have Ah evah done to you to merit such treatment at yoh hands?'

"I see there's no use to lie to him, so I gives it to him straight.

"'Mr. Sanford,' I says, 'the hoss can't win without it, 'n' I don't want to see you lose your money.'

"Ole man Sanford sort-a wilts. He seems to get smaller. I've never noticed how old he is till now. He stands a-lookin' at me like he never sees me before.

"The crowd begins to yell as the hosses hit the stretch. The Tramp is out in front, 'n' he stays there all the way.

"The ole man never even looks towards the track.

"'He wins easy,' says Chick as they go under the wire, 'n' all you can hear is 'Trampfast! Trampfast!' but ole man Sanford still keeps a-starin' at me.

"'You want to cheer up, Mr. Sanford,' I says. 'You win a nice bet on him.'

"He pulls the tickets out of his pocket 'n' looks at 'em. They call fur sixteen hundred bucks.

"'As Ah have told you once befoh, young man,' he says, a-lookin' at the tickets. 'Ah can not blame you greatly, because you are paht of yoh times. This is the excuse Ah find foh you in thinking Ah would value money moh than the spohts-manship of a gentleman. Yoh times are bad, young man!' he says. 'They have succeeded in staining the puhple and white at the vehy end. Ah would neveh have raced afteh to-day. It was a whim of an old man to see his colohs once moh among a field of hawses. Ah knew Ah was not of this day. Ah should have known bettah than to become a paht of it even foh a little time. Ah have learned ma lesson,' he says, lookin' up at me. 'But you have made it vehy bittah.'

"He looks down at the tickets again fur a minute. . . Then he tears 'em across three ways 'n' drops 'em on the ground."

CLASS

"What do you like in the handicap?" I asked, looking up from the form sheet.

Blister reached for the paper.

"Indigo's the class," he said, after a glance at the entries. "If they run to form, he'll cop."

"There you go again - with your *class*!" I exclaimed. "You're always talking about class. What does class mean?"

"Long as you've been hangin' 'round the track 'n' not know what class means!" Blister looked at me pityingly. "There's no *class* to that," he added, with a grin.

"Seriously now," I urged. "Explain it to me. Class, as you call it, is beaten right along. Just the other day you said Exponent was the class and should have won, but he didn't."

"He has the most left at that," said Blister. "He wins in three more jumps. You can't beat class. It'll come back fur more."

"Molly S. beat him," I insisted.

"Yep, she beat him that one race," Blister admitted. "But how does she beat him? Do you notice the boy gets her away wingin' 'n' keeps her there all the trip? . . . Why? Because he knows she can't come from behind 'n' win. If the old hoss gets

John Taintor Foote

to her any place in the stretch she lays down to him sure. She ain't got the class 'n' he has. She can win a race now 'n' then when things break right fur her, but the Exponent hoss'll win anyway - on three legs if he has to. He's got the class."

"How can you get horses with class?" I inquired. "By breeding?"

"If you want it you lay down big coin fur it," Blister answered. "It follows blood lines some, but not all the time. I've seed awful dogs bred clear to the clouds. Then again it'll show in a weanlin'. I've seed sucklin' colts with class stickin' out all over 'em. Kids has it, too. It shows real young sometimes."

"How can a child show anything like that?" I remonstrated. "He has no opportunity. Class, as I understand it, is deep-seated - part of the very fiber. It takes a big situation to bring it out. Where did you ever see a child display this quality?"

"I've seed it many a time in little dirty-faced swipes," Blister stated. "I've seed exercise-boys so full of class they put the silks on 'em before they can bridle a hoss, 'n' they bawl like you've took away their apple when they lose their first race. You've heard of Hamilton?"

"I have been told he is the best sire in America," I replied, wondering where this question led.

"I won't say that," said Blister. "There's a lot of good hosses at stud in this land-of-the-free-when-you-pay-fur-it, but he's up there with the best of 'em. Did you know I owns him once myself?"

"Not the great Hamilton?" I protested.

"Yep, the great all-the-time, anyhow-'n'-any-place Hamilton," Blister assured me. "'N' speakin' of class in kids 'n' colts, lemme tell you about it." He reached for his "makin's" and I waited while he rolled a cigarette, this process being a necessary prelude to a journey into his past.

"The year Seattle Sam goes down 'n' out," the words came in a cloud of cigarette smoke, "I'm at Saratoga. This Seattle is one of the big plungers, his nod's good with the bookies fur anything he wants to lay, 'n' he sure bets 'em to the sky. He owns a grand string of hosses, 'n' when one of 'em's out to win, believe me, he carries the coin!"

"All the same they get him at last 'n' there ain't nothin' else talked about fur a couple of days when the word goes 'round that he's cleaned. The bunch acts like somebody's dead. They whisper when they tell it. It's got 'em dazed.

"In them days there's a little squirt called Micky that hangs around the track. He ain't got a regular job; he just picks up odd mounts on a work-out now 'n' then. He don't weigh eighty pounds, but he's fresher'n a bucket of paint. His right name's Vincent Mulligan, 'n' his mother's a widow woman. I learns that 'cause the old lady sends a truant officer out to the track after him one day, 'n' the cop puts me wise after Micky has clumb through a stall window, 'n' give him the slip.

"'Why, you big truck hoss,' says Micky to the bull as he skidoos through the window, 'you couldn't catch a cold at the north pole in yer dirty undershirt!'

"'Why don't you go to school like you'd ought, Vincent?' I says to Micky, when he shows up the next day.

"'Aw, you go to hell!' says Micky. 'Say, are you ever goin' to let me work one of yer dogs out in place of that smoke?' he says, pointin' at Snowball, my exercise-boy.

"'Who you callin' a smoke?' says Snowball, startin' fur Micky. 'I'll slap the ugly I'ish mouth off you!'

"Micky picks up a pitchfork.

"'Go awn, you black boob!' he says. 'If I reaches fer yer gizzard with this tickler, I gets it!'

"Snowball backs up. I grabs the fork from the little shrimp.

"'Now, you beat it!' I says to him.

"'Aw, you go to hell!' says Micky. He lays down on a bail of straw 'n' pulls his hat over his face. 'If any guy bothers me while I'm gettin' my rest,' he says, 'call a hearse. Don't wake me up till some guy wants a hoss worked out.'

"One day I goes to lay a piker's bet in Ike Rosenberg's book.

"'All across on Tantrum,' I says to Ike.

"'Hello, Blister,' says Ike, when he goes to hand me the ticket. 'I like that one myself. Go over 'n' lay me a hundred 'n' fifty the same way, - here's the change.'

"When I bring Ike his ticket he tells me to wait a minute, 'n' pretty soon he puts a sheet-writer on the block 'n' steps down.

"'Come over here,' he says, 'n' I trails him out of the bettin' shed. 'I've took a two-year-old for a thousand dollar marker of Seattle's,' says Ike, swingin' 'round on me. 'You want him?'

"'To train, you mean?' I says, 'Is that it?'

"'Sure,' says Ike. 'You can have him on shares if you want.'

"'Tell me about him,' I says.

"'Well,' says Ike, 'he's a big little hoss made good all over. He ain't never started yet, but he's been propped for two months. He's by Edgemont. First dam, Cora, by Musketeer. Second dam, Debutante, by Peddler. Third dam, Daisy Dean, by Salvation. Fourth dam, Iole, by Messenger. He's registered as Hamilton, 'n' that's all I know.'

"'That's sure some breedin',' I says. 'But I never takes a colt on shares. I'll handle him fur you as careful as I know how 'n' it'll cost you fifty a month. That's the best I can do.'

"'I'll send him over this evenin',' says Ike. 'Let me know what you think of him after he works out for you.'

"I like this Hamilton colt the minute I gets my lamps on him. He ain't over fifteen hands, but he's all hoss. He'll weigh right at nine hundred, 'n' that's quite a chunk of a two-year-old. He's got a fine little head on him 'n' his eye has the right look. A good game hoss'll look at you like a eagle. I don't want nothin' to do with a sheep-eyed pup. This colt has a eye like a game cock.

"Peewee Simpson is at my stalls when they brings the colt over, 'n' after we've sized him up I asks Peewee what he thinks of the little rooster.

"'Him?' says Peewee. 'He's a bear-cat. I'll bet he entertains you frequent 'n' at short notice. I don't figger him related to Mary's lamb, not any. You better keep your eye on little Hamilton. Hammy's likely to be a naughty boy any time.'

"Peewee's got the correct hunch - the first time Snowball takes him out Hamilton runs off 'n' the boy don't get him stopped till he romps five miles.

"'Can't you stop him sooner'n that?' I says to Snowball when he's back.

"Micky's at the stalls that mawnin', 'n' he butts in, as usual.

"'Stop him!' he says. 'That black boob couldn't stop a hoss in a box stall. Lemme me have him next work-out!'

"'I'll let you have a slap on the ear,' I says.

"'Aw, you go to hell!' says Micky.

John Taintor Foote

"Next work-out day Hamilton pulls off the same stunt. He's feelin' extra good that mawnin', I guess, 'cause he makes a nine mile trip of it. Micky stands there with me, watchin' the colt go round 'n' round the track.

"'Why don't you can that choc'lit drop,' he says, "'n' put a white man up?'

"'Meanin' you?' I says. 'You'd holler fur your milk bottle before he goes a eighth with you.'

"'Aw, you go to hell!' says Micky.

"I borrows a curb 'n' chain from Eddy Murphy - he's been usin' it on ole Dandelion. It's fierce - you can bust a hoss's jaw with it. I puts it on Hamilton next work-out.

"'I guess that'll hold little Hammy,' I says, when Snowball's up. But it don't. The colt ain't any more'n felt the curb when he bolts into the fence 'n' chucks Snowball off. I starts to catch the hoss, but Micky gets to him first 'n' grabs him.

"'Lemme give him a whirl,' he says. 'Come on - be a sport fur a change!'

"Snowball rolls away from the colt 'n' picks hisself up.

"'He is shoh welcome to him,' he says. 'I got no moh use foh him.'

"I studies a minute, lookin' at Micky. He don't come much above Hamilton's knee. He's lookin' at me like a pup beggin' fur a bone.

"'Go to it, you ornery little shrimp!' I says at last. 'If a worse pair ever gets together I've never seed it!'

"Micky gives a yelp like a terrier.

"'Take off this bit 'n' put a straight bar on him,' he says.

"'Why, you couldn't hold one of his ears with a bar bit,' I says.

"'Who's ridin' this hoss?' says Micky. 'Go awn, get the bit!'

"'Get him what he wants,' I says to Snowball.

"We leads the colt on to the track, when the bits is changed, 'n' just as I throws Micky up I see he's got a bat.

"'What you goin' to do with that?' I says. 'You need a parachute, not a whip!'

"'*I* always ride 'em with a bat. Turn him loose,' says Micky.

"Well, it's the same thing over again, the colt runs off. All Micky does is to keep him in the track. I see he ain't pullin' a pound. They've gone about six mile 'n' Hamilton begins to slow a little. Just then Micky lights into him with the bat.

"'Look at dat!' says Snowball. 'He's los' his min'.'

"'*No, he ain't!*' I says. '*He's there forty ways!*' I've just begun to tumble the kid's wise as owls. 'Oh, you Micky!' I hollers. 'Go to it, you white boy!'

"I hate to tell you how far that kid works the hoss. He keeps handin' him the bat every other jump. It gets so I can run as fast as they're movin' 'n' Hamilton's just prayin' fur help. I'm afraid he'll jim the colt fur good, so I yells at Micky to cut it out, when he comes by.

"'Come down off of that, you squirt!' I says. 'Do you want to kill the colt?'

"'Aw, you go to hell!' he says, 'n' 'round they go again. When Hamilton ain't got more'n a good stagger left, Micky rides him through the gate to the stall.

"'Now, pony,' he says to Hamilton, 'don't start nothin' you can't finish.'

"The trip kills a ordinary hoss, but they ain't nothin' ordinary about this Hamilton. I learns *that* then. We cools him out good 'n' in three days he's kickin' the roof off the stall.

"Come work-out day Micky goes up on Hamilton. Say, the colt eats out of his hand. Micky's got him buffaloed right. He gallops Hamilton a nice mile 'n' pulls up at the gate.

"'What do you want him to do now? Stand on his head?' he says. 'Times is dull.'

"'Shoot him three furlongs,' I says.

"'Shoot is the word,' says Micky.

"Hamilton romps the three furlongs in nothin' flat - I'm tickled sick.

"'He's a bear!' I says to Micky at the stalls. "N' as fur you - you're on the pay-roll.'

"'Why, you're a live one, ain't you?' says Micky. 'Wait till I go chase the Smoke!' The next thing I see is Snowball goin' down the line like a quarter hoss, 'n' Micky's proddin' at him with a pitchfork.

"'He won't be back,' says Micky, when he's puttin' up the fork.

"'Now, look-a here,' I says, 'you got to cut this rough stuff, if you works fur me.'

"'Aw, you go to hell!' says Micky to me.

"Right then I gets him by the collar, 'n' takes a bat from the rack. I works on him till the bat's wore out 'n' then reaches fur another. Micky ain't opened his face. I wears that one out 'n' grabs another. Micky looks up at the rack - there's four more bats left.

"'Nix on number three!' he yells. 'I'm listenin' to you!'

"'All right,' I says, hangin' up the bat. 'Now, listen good. *Cut out this rough stuff* - you got me?'

"'I got you,' says Micky.

"I tells Ike he's got a good colt, but only one boy can ride him. Ike comes over to the stalls with me to see the boy 'n' Hamilton.

"'Not that kid?' he says, when he takes a slant at Micky. 'A hobby-hoss lets him out.'

"Micky goes straight up.

"'Why, you fat-headed Kike!' he says. 'The only thing you can tell me about a hoss is how much the nails cost to hold his shoes on.'

"Ike turns to me.

"'Don't never let that boy throw a leg over a hoss of mine again,' he says. 'Enter this colt in the two-year-old scramble Friday. I'll get Whitman to ride. I guess *he'll* hold him.'

"'Now, look at that!' I says to Micky when Ike's gone. 'You *will* shoot off your face, won't you? Ain't you *never* goin' to learn to keep that loud trap of yours closed?'

"'Aw, you go -' Micky stops there.

"I takes a step towards the whip rack.

"'Come on -' I says, 'let's hear from you!'

"'- to hell with the big Kike!' says Micky.

"'Does that let me in?' I says.

"Micky studies a minute lookin' at me 'n' the bats in the rack.

"'Naw - just the Kike,' he says at last.

"When Whitman's up on Hamilton, before they goes to the post, I tries to put him wise.

"'You're on a bad actor, Whitty,' I says. 'If you ain't on your toes, he runs off with you sure.' This Whitman's a star, 'n' nobody knows it better'n him.

"'What do *you* hire a jock fur?' he says. 'Why don't you train 'n' ride both?'

"'All right,' I says. 'I'm *tellin'* you now!'

"'If this hoss is ready,' says Whitman, 'you've earned your money - don't work overtime.'

"I goes through the paddock 'n' out on the lawn. Before I'm there I hears the crowd yellin'. When I can see the track, there's the field at the post all but Hamilton. He 'n' Whitty has made a race all to theirselves. It turns out to be a six mile ramble with only one entry.

"I goes to the stand 'n' scratches Hamilton while he's still runnin'. The field waits at the post till they get a clear track.

"'I didn't know this was a distance race,' I says to Whitty when he gets down. Whitty's sore as a crab, the bunch'll mention it to him the rest of the season.

"'You don't want a jock on this thing,' he says. 'A engineer is what he needs.'

"'Sell him,' is the first words Ike says to me when I sees him.

"'*Sell him?*' I says. 'You must be drunk! Why, he don't bring a ten case note. Everybody's hep he's a bolter. Now listen! This is a real good colt, 'n' I know it; but the bunch don't. That boy of mine can ride him. If you gives the colt another chance with my boy up, he shows 'em somethin'. Then you can get a price fur him.'

"'Do what you like with him,' says Ike. 'But I don't pay out another simoleon on him! I'm through right now!'

"'Give me half what he wins his next out 'n' *I'll* take a chance with him,' I says.

"'You're on,' says Ike. 'But you pay the entrance.'

"'Surest thing you know,' I says, 'n' goes over to the stalls.

"In two weeks there's to be a handicap fur two-year-olds. It's worth three thousand to the winner. It's the best baby race at the meetin'. Hamilton'll come in awful light 'n' he'll get five pounds apprentice allowance fur Micky; but it'll put a big crimp in my roll to pay the entrance. I studies over it some 'n' I gets cold feet. It takes three hundred bones to sit in. I've about decided it's too rich fur my blood, when next work-out day comes 'n' Hamilton works four furlongs, with Micky up, like a cyclone. That gets my circulation goin' 'n' I takes a shot at it.

"'Who's burning this up on the ten mile wonder?' says the sec. to me, when I'm payin' the entrance. 'The work seems a little coarse for my old friend Ike.'

"'I'm Smiling Faces this load of poles,' I says.

"'Why, Blister,' says the sec. 'I never thought it of you! But we're much obliged to you just the same.'

John Taintor Foote

"There's eight starters in the handicap besides Hamilton. One of 'em's a big clumsy colt named Hellespont. The bunch calls him the Elephant, 'n' he's sour as lemons. I see his eyes a-rollin' in the paddock, 'n' I know he's hopped. Just as the parade starts he begins to cut the mustard. He rears 'n' tries to come down all spraddled out on the colt ahead of him in the line, but the jock runs him into a stall 'n' they take hold of him till the rest is out on the track.

"Micky ain't had no experience at the post. I've borrowed a pair of glasses 'n' I'm watchin' the get-a-way pretty anxious. Hamilton's actin' fine, but the Elephant is holdin' up the start. All of a sudden he rears clear up 'n' comes down across Hamilton. The colt does a flop 'n' I see the Elephant rear 'n' stamp him a couple a times before the assistant drives him off with the bull whip."

"'Good-by, three hundred!' I says to myself, I can't see good fur the dust, but they pulls Micky out from under the colt, 'n' when I gets another slant, Hamilton's on his feet 'n' the starter's talkin' at Micky. I can see Micky shakin' his head. It ain't long till they puts him up again.

"'That's the good game kid!' I says out loud. 'Oh, you 'Micky boy!' also out loud.

"They get off to a nice start. When they hit the stretch I throws my hat away. Hamilton's in front two lengths. A eighth from home I see there's somethin' wrong with Micky. He's got his bat 'n' lines in his left mitt. His right hook is kind-a floppin' at his side, but Hamilton's runnin' true 'n' strong. The colt looks awful good to the sixteenth 'n' then his gait goes clear to the bad. I see he's all shot to pieces behind, 'n' he's stoppin' fast. I'm standin' at the inner rail ten len'ths from the wire, 'n' the Elephant colt gets to Hamilton right in front of me.

"'I gotcha, jock!' yells the boy on the Elephant.

"'They don't pay off here,' says Micky, 'n' sticks the lines in his face. Then he goes to the bat with his south hook 'n' Hamilton lays back his ears 'n' runs true again. . . . He out-games the Elephant a nod at the wire 'n' I'm twelve hundred to the clear.

"When I gets to 'em, Micky's standin' in the track leanin' against Hamilton. The colt's shakin' all over 'n' his hind feet's in a big pool of blood. I gives a' look 'n' the left rear tendon is tore off from hock to fetlock.

"'Good God, look at that!' I says to Micky.

"Micky turns 'n' looks.

"'Aw, pony . . .' he says, 'n' busts out cryin'. He leans up against the colt again 'n' he's shakin' as bad as Hamilton.

"Just then the boy gets down from the Elephant.

"'I'd a beat that dog in another jump,' he says to Micky.

"'You?' says Micky. 'I'm goin' to *kill you!*' He starts fur the boy, but he turns kind-a greeny white 'n' does a flop on the track.

"When I goes to pick him up I see a bone comin' through the flesh just above the wrist on his right hook.

"We puts him in a blanket 'n' the swipes start to carry him off.

"'What's the matter with the kid?' says Ike comin' up.

"'Arm broke, I guess,' I says."

"Ike sees the blood 'n' walks behind Hamilton.

"'I wish it was his neck,' he says, pointin' at the tendon. 'That's what you get fur puttin' a pin-headed apprentice on a good hoss! Get him so he can hobble, 'n' sell him to a livery if you can. If not, have him shot.'

"Hamilton's standin' there a-shakin'. His eyes has the look you always sees in a hoss just after he's ruined.

"'What'll you take fur him?' I says to Ike.

"'Take fur him?' he says. 'Whatever he'll bring. I ain't out nothin' on him. I splits three thousand with you to the race.'

"'You owe me a hundred 'n' thirty fur trainin',' I says. 'I calls it off 'n' keeps the hoss.'

"'You've bought him,' says Ike, 'n' goes back to the bettin' shed.

"They take Micky to the hospital. The doc says his arm's broke 'n' he's hurt inside. He comes to before they puts him in the ambulance.

"'Why didn't you let another boy ride?' says the assistant starter, who's helpin' the doc.

"'Ride hell!' says Micky. 'He runs off with them other boobs.'

"Me 'n' Peewee Simpson gets Hamilton to the stall. It takes him just one hour to do that hundred yards, but I've got a tight bandage above the hock 'n' he don't bleed so bad.

"'Can you get him so he can walk?' I says to the vet. when he's looked at the colt.

"'Yes,' he says; 'but that'll be about all for him. I advise you to have him destroyed. What hoss *is* this?'

"'Hamilton,' I says. 'He just wins the colt race.'

"'So?' he says. 'I didn't see it. When did *this* happen?'

"'At the post,' I says. 'Another colt jumped on him.'

"'At the post?' he says. 'I thought you said he won?'

"'He did,' I says.

"'On *that?*' he says, pointin' to the leg. 'What you tryin' to do, kid me?'

"'I'm tellin' it to you just as she happens,' I says. 'It don't matter a damn to me whether you believe it or not!'

"'Why, you *ain't* kiddin', are you?' he says. 'Wait a minute -'

"He goes outside 'n' I see him talkin' to several.

"'It's straight,' he says, when he comes back. 'But it ain't possible!'

"'Who owns this colt?' he says, after he's looked at the leg some more.

"'I do,' I says. 'I just give a hundred 'n' thirty fur him.'

"'What did you ever buy *him* for?' he says.

"I studies a minute, a-lookin' at Hamilton.

"'I've got softenin' of the brain, I guess,' I says.

"'He's a nice made thing,' says the vet. 'How's he bred?'

"I tells him, 'n' he looks at the leg some more, 'n' then walks 'round the colt a couple a times.

"'I tell you what I'll do,' he says after while. 'I'll take him off your hands at just what you paid. I'm givin' it to you straight - *this hoss wont never do more than walk.* But he's bred out a sight 'n' I like his looks. There's a chance somebody could use him

John Taintor Foote

in the stud. I'm willin' to get him in some sort-a shape 'n' see if I can't make a piece of money on him. What do you say?"

"'Well,' I says, 'you're fixed better to get him in shape'n me. I just wanted to give the little hoss a show. If *you'll* give it to him, he's yours.'

"'Here's your money,' says the vet. 'I'll send my wagon for him to-morrow. Let me have a lantern till I get this leg so it won't hurt him so bad to-night.'

"The next day every paper I picks up has a great big write-up in it about Micky 'n' the colt. Until the wagon comes fur him there's a regular procession to the stall to look at Hamilton, 'n' when I goes to the hospital that night you can't see Micky fur flowers around his bed.

"'Hell!' says Micky. 'Do they think I'm a stiff?'

"'Sh-h-h!' says the sister that's nursin' him.

"I don't see Hamilton fur a month. One day I goes over to the big Eastern sale at New York, just to hear ole Pappy Danforth sell 'em. Pappy's stood on a block all his life. He knows every hoss-man in the country. When *he* tells you about a hoss, it's right; 'n' everybody takes his tip. He just about sells 'em where they ought to go.

"There's a fierce crowd at the sale 'n' some grand stuff goes under the hammer. Pappy kids the crowd along 'n' sells 'em so fast it makes you dizzy. They don't more'n lead a hoss out till he's gone.

"All of a sudden Pappy climbs clear up on the desk in front of him 'n' stands there a minute, pushin' back his long white hair.

"'Na-ow, boys!' he says. 'I'm goin' to sell you a three-legged hoss!' An' - listen to the ole man - he's wuth more'n any four-legged hoss, livin' or dead!'

"I rubbers hard to get a look at a hoss Pappy boosts like that, 'n' I nearly croaks when they lead Hamilton into the ring. The colt's a dink, right. He's stiff as a poker behind, but he's still got that game-cock look to his eye.

"'Na-ow, boys!' sings out Pappy, 'there's the biggest little hoss ever you saw! Don't look at him - any of you fellahs that wants a yellah dawg to win a cheap race with! *He* ain't in *that* class. Step forwahd, you breeders, an' grasp a golden opportunity! Send the best brood mares you've got to this little hoss . . . he's a giant! *You hear me - a giant!* Ed Tumble, I'm talkin' to you! I'm talkin' to you, Bill Masters - an' Harry Scott there . . . an' Judge Dillon . . . an' all you big breeders! You've *read* what this little hoss done in the newspapers. You can *see* his breedin' in your catalogues. You can *look him over* as he stands there! But best of all - *listen to the old man!* when he tells you he never held a hammer over a better one in fifty years. Na-ow, boys! I'm goin' to sell him for the high dollah, an' the man who gets him at any price . . . *you hear me - at any price!* . . . is goin' to have the laugh on the rest of you fellahs! Aw-l-l right - *what do I hear?'*

"'Five hundred!' says some guy.

"'Why, Frank, five hundred won't buy a hair out of his tail . . . *what do I hear?'* says Pappy.

"'Two thousand!' yells somebody.

"'Na-ow listen, Tom, if you want the little hoss, cut out this triflin' an' bid for him,' says Pappy. '*What do I hear?'*

"'Five thousand!' some guy hollers.

"'That's just a nice little start . . . *what do I hear?'* says Pappy, 'n' I goes into a trance.

John Taintor Foote

"I don't come to till I hears Pappy sing out:

"'So-o-ld to you for sixteen thousand dollahs, Mr. Humphrey, *an' you never bought a cheaper one!*'

"It's a wonder I ain't run over gettin' to the depot. I don't know where I'm at. I just keeps sayin' 'sixteen thousand - sixteen thousand - ' over 'n' over to myself. I beats it out to the hospital when I gets back, to tell Micky. They're goin' to let him out in a day or so 'n' Micky's settin' up in a chair with wheels to it.

"'Give a guess what Hamilton brings in the Big Eastern,' I says to him.

"'I dunno,' says he. 'How much?'

"'Sixteen thousand bucks!' I says. 'How does that lay on your stummick?'

"'Hell!' says Micky. 'That ain't nothin' - look-a-here!'

"He shoves a paper at me he's been holdin' in his mitt. It's a ridin' contract fur two years with the Ogden stable at ten thousand a year.

"So you see, just like I tells you," Blister wound up, "they lay down real money fur *class*."

"The man who bought the horse," I said, "certainly got what he paid for - everybody knows *now* that Hamilton has class. But how about the boy?"

"Did you ever see Vincent ride?" Blister looked at me inquiringly.

"I saw him ride once in the English Derby," I replied. "Why?"

"Well," said Blister, "his mother lives in New York in a

brownstone house he bought her, with two Swede girls to do as much work as she'll let 'em. When he comes home, she calls him 'Micky.' Is there class to him?"

"Yes," I said, "there's class to him."

EXIT BUTSY

"What's all them rubes got ribbons on 'em fur?" asked Blister.

I followed his gaze to a group of variously garbed men and women who had just rounded the paddock, and who slowly bore down upon us as they drifted from stall to stall in a haphazard inspection of the great racing plant at Latonia. Prominent upon the person of each member of this party was a bountiful strip of yellow ribbon. The effect was decidedly gay.

I had encountered similar ribbons in every nook and cranny of the Queen City during the last few days, and I knew that each bore in thirty-six point Gothic condensed, the words, "Ohio State Grange."

"Those are Ohio farmers and their wives who are attending a convention in Cincinnati," I explained. "The ribbons are convention badges."

Blister allowed the saddle girth he was mending to lie unnoticed across his knees as the delegates by twos and threes straggled past.

Each female member of the party carried a round paper fan with a cane handle, and talked unceasingly. These streams of conversation were entirely regardless of one another. It was as though many brooks babbled onward side by side, but never joined. One fragment that reached us, I preserved.

"An' I sez to the doctor when he come, sez I, 'Doctor, I ain't held a bite on my stummick these three livelong days!'" This was delivered by a buxom dame, fanning vigorously the meanwhile, and was noteworthy since the lady was closely followed by a little man whose frailty suggested dissolution, and who bore a large lunch box under one arm and a heavy child upon the other.

The men appeared somewhat interested in the pampered nervous-looking thoroughbreds, but made few comments. As compared to their women folk they seemed more silent than the very tomb itself.

Long after the grangers had drifted out of our sight, Blister's thoughts seemed devoted to them. Several times he chuckled to himself.

"Every time I see a bunch of rubes," he said at last, "it puts me in mind of Butsy Trimble 'n' the new stalls at Lake Minnehaha Park."

"Lake Minnehaha Park," I repeated. "I never heard of such a place."

"It's up at Mount Clinton," Blister explained. "It's Ohio's beauty spot."

"Get out!" I scoffed.

"Fact!" said Blister. "It says so right over the gates."

"Tell me about it," I demanded.

"This ain't been so long ago," said Blister. "The meetin' here at Latonia is about over. Ole Whiskers has put the game on the fritz in New York, so everybody's studyin' where to ship when get-away day comes, 'n' the whole bunch is sore as bears - you can't get a pleasant word from nobody.

"All I got in my string is some two-year-olds of Judge Dillon's. They go back to the farm when the meetin' closes, so I ain't worried none - not about where to ship.

"One night me 'n' Peewee Simpson is playin' pitch on a bale of hay with a lantern. Butsy Trimble is settin' beside the bale readin' a hoss paper.

"'Gimme high, jack, game - ' says Peewee, after a hand.

"'I'll give you a poke in the nose!' I says. 'What you got fur game?'

"'I s'pose you want to count fur game - don't you?' says Peewee. 'I'll give it to you sooner'n argue with you.'

"'You're right, you'll give it to me,' I says.

"'Well, I said I'd give it to you, didn't I?' says Peewee. 'You'd rather argue'n eat, wouldn't you?'

"'All that's wrong with you,' I says, 'is you're sore 'cause you can't hog game!'

"Peewee lays down his cards.

"'Now, look a here, you freckle-faced shrimp!' he says. 'Get off this bale of hay - it'll *poison* a hoss if *you* set on it much longer!'

"'Whose bale of hay do you think this is?' I says. 'You tryin' to hog *it* like you does game?'

"'Gimme my lantern 'n' I'll be on my way,' says Peewee.

"'I puts the oil in that lantern,' I says, ''n' she sets right where she is till she makes her last flicker.'

"'Cut it! Cut it!' says Butsy, spreadin' out his hoss paper. 'Act like you has some sense, 'n' I puts you hep to a hot scheme I gets out of this paper - us three can pull it off to a finish!'

"'I don't want in on no scheme with that lantern snatcher!' says Peewee then to me.

"'If you don't age some,' I says to Peewee, 'nursie'll come around here, 'n' put a nice fresh panty-waist on you!'

"Then Butsy goes ahead 'n' tells us the frame-up. He shows us an ad in his paper askin' fur entries to race over the Ohio Short Ship Circuit. This circuit is a bunch of race meets that's held on the bull rings at county fairs up through the state. They're trottin' races mostly, but they give one runnin' race at a different town each week.

"'Now,' says Butsy, 'I'm born 'n' raised in Mount Clinton, Ohio. I sees the race meet there frequent 'n' she's a peach. You can have a hoss lay down 'n' go to sleep on the track if you don't want him to win 'n' then tell the judges he's got spring fever. Everything goes except murder. We'll take that black stud of mine 'n' Peewee's bay geldin' 'n' hit this punkin circuit. We can win a purse each week fur travelin' expenses, 'n' what we cops on the side is velvet.'

"'What do you want me fur?' I says.

"'Why,' says Butsy, 'at these county fairs there ain't no bookies. They just bets from hand to hand. While me 'n' Peewee rides, you sashay out among the rubes 'n' get the coin down on whichever hoss we frames to win.'

"We sets there 'n' talks over the proposition most all night. Butsy says it's a cinch 'n' it ain't long till me 'n' Peewee figgers he's got it doped right.

"'Let's go against it, Blister,' Peewee says to me. 'What do you say, old pal?'

"'I'm there with bells on,' I says, 'n' that settles it. I ships my

John Taintor Foote

colts to Judge Dillon, 'n' the next week we start.

"These punkin races is all half-mile dashes, best two out of three. Peewee's geldin' is a distance hoss - he don't get goin' good under a mile. In a bull-ring sprint he ain't got a chance with this black stud of Butsy's.

"Our game is to have Butsy turn his dash-hound loose the first heat. Then I ambulates out among the rubes 'n' acts like I'm willing to bet on the bay geldin'. If I finds a live one, Butsy takes his hoss up in his lap the last two trips 'n' Peewee comes on 'n' grabs the gravy.

"We figger the rubes'll eat it up after seein' that nice-lookin' black stud romp away with the first heat. But right there the dope falls down - the rubes ain't as dead as they look.

"In the first town we strike I eases up to a tall Jasper after the black hoss has grabbed the opener on the bit.

"'Say, pardner,' I says, 'do you ever bet a piece of money on a race?'

"This Jasper is just a Adam's apple surrounded by arms 'n' legs.

"'Well, I should say as much,' he says. 'But most ginrally they wan't nobody bet with me. Up in Liberty Township the boys call me Lucky Andy.'

"'It's a crime to do this!' I says to myself. 'I'll make a little bet with you, pardner,' I says out loud. 'Not much though - you're too lucky!'

"'How was ye calkewlatin' to bet?' says the Jasper.

"'This black hoss acted kind-a tired to me,' I says. 'I'll just bet you twenty bucks he don't win the race.'

"'You look like a smart little cuss,' he says. 'What's good

enough fer you is good enough fer me.' He beats it over to where another rube is settin' in a buggy. 'Hi, Bill!' says my Jasper, 'I'll just bet ye fifty cents the black hawse dun't win the race - even if I do lose!'

"That's the way it goes right along - the rubes stay away from it. Once in a while I finds a mark but not often. We win a purse though in every town 'n' this just about pays expenses. We ain't makin' nothin' much, but we ain't losin' nothin' neither. We're eatin' regular 'n' enjoyin' ourselves, except Butsy. *He* wouldn't enjoy hisself at a dog fight.

"This Butsy Trimble is a thin solemn gink 'n' he almost never cracks a smile. He's got it doped out that everybody's agin him. Peewee 'n' me has knocked around together so much we knows each other's ways, but we ain't never had much to do with this Butsy, so we ain't wise to him at first.

"It ain't long till Butsy begins to figger we're tryin' to hand it to him. He gets sour-balled about everythin' we does. We try to kid him, but he ain't hep to a kid 'n' he don't stand fur it like he'd ought. His favorite stunt is to say he'll take his hoss 'n' quit. He springs this right along.

"From the start this trip gets to Peewee's funny bone. He don't do nothin' but laugh. Butsy don't see nothin' funny about it, 'n' he gets to thinkin' Peewee's laughin' at him.

"Peewee'll lay in the stall at night 'n' laugh 'n' laugh. Pretty soon he'll get me goin', 'n' then we'll lay 'n' snort fur a hour. Butsy can't go to sleep 'n' he gets wild.

"'What th' hell are you laughin' at?' he says. 'If you don't cut this out 'n' let me get my rest I'll quit the game tomorrow!'

"It gets so I don't dare look at Peewee fur fear we'll get started 'n' Butsy'll quit.

"At a burg called Mansfield I finds a good bunch of live ones 'n' we grabs off three hundred life-savers. It seems to help Butsy a lot - he acts more cheerful right away.

"'Cherries are ripe,' he says. 'Our next town's Mount Clinton. I know every boob in it. We'll sift some change out of them Knox County plow-pushers.'

"We ships over the B. & O. to Mount Clinton. It's rainin' when we unloads, 'n' Butsy ain't as cheerful as he was.

"'How far is it to the track?' Peewee says to him.

"'About three miles 'n' all hills,' says Butsy.

"'How do you get out?' says Peewee.

"'We could take the street-car if it wasn't fur the hosses,' says Butsy. 'As it is we'll have to hoof it through the mud.'

"'Look-a here,' I says to Butsy, 'there's no sense in three of us gettin' wet. You know the way 'n' we don't. You take the hosses 'n' we'll come out on the street-car.'

"'I thought it 'ud be like that,' says Butsy. 'You two always pick out the soft stuff fur yourselves 'n' hand me the lemons. I guess I'll just put my hoss back in the freight car 'n' be on my way.'

"'Now, Butsy,' I says, 'have some sense! We ain't slippin' you nothin'. I'd take the dogs 'n' leave you 'n' Peewee ride if I knew the way. What do you want to make a crack about quittin' fur just as the game's gettin' good?' I says. 'We cops a neat little bundle at our last stop, 'n' we'll grab a nice piece of change here. I feel it in my bones.'

"'All right,' says Butsy. 'I'll be the goat just once more - but take it from me this is the last time!'

"'Send a wagon fur the trunk when you get up-town,' I says to

Butsy when he's goin'.

"'Furget it!' he says. 'Put her on the street-car. The car runs right into Minnehaha Park 'n' you can unload her in front of the stalls.'

"'You can't take a trunk on a street-car,' I says.

"'Wait till you see this street-car,' says Butsy.

"'Ain't they but one?' says Peewee.

"'That's all,' says Butsy. 'Orphy Shanner runs it.'

"Me and Peewee stands a-waitin' fur the street-car fur thirty minutes, then I goes into the freight depot office.

"'Is the street-car runnin'?' I says to the old gazink at the desk.

"'Ye can't rightly call it runnin',' he says. 'It ain't been settled yet. Some claims she dun't, some claims she do. Them that claims she dun't is those who've rid on her.'

"'Well, whatever she does,' I says, 'will she get here this mawnin'? I got to get to the race track.'

"'I'll call up Orphy an' see,' says the old gazink. 'Hello, Tessie,' he says, after he grinds away at the telephone handle fur a while. 'Git a-holt of Orphy Shanner fer me out to th' park - that's a good girl.' In about ten minutes somebody begins to talk over the phone. 'Say, Orphy, this is Ed at the B. & O. Freight,' says the old gazink. 'I got a passenger down here fer ye.' Then he listens at the phone. 'I don't know who he is. He's a stranger tu me,' he says, 'n' listens some more. 'All right, I'll tell him,' he says, 'n' hangs up the phone.

"'Orphy says fer me to tell ye thet he's comin' in to get Mrs. Boone at the Public Square at eleven o'clock,' he says to me. 'He's goin' to take her out High Street to a whisk party at Mrs.

Pucker's, an' he'll come down here an' git ye then.'

"'Why, it ain't ten o'clock yet,' I says.

"'Well, you kin set in here out of the rain an' wait,' he says.

"I thinks we better walk 'n' then I remembers that cussed trunk.

"'Much obliged,' I says. 'I'll go out 'n' get my friend.'

"'Be they two of ye?' says he. 'Jeerusalem, I told Orphy they wa'n't but one.'

"When I gets back with Peewee, the old gazink pushes a couple of chairs at us.

"'Set right down, boys,' he says, "n' make yourselves mis'able.' Then he puts a chew in his face that would choke a he-elephant 'n' begins to ask us questions. The only thing he don't ask us he don't think of. He'll stop right in the middle of a word 'n' say, 'pit-too-ee,' 'n' hit a flat box full of sawdust dead center. I don't see him miss once.'

"After he's got us pumped dry he begins to tell us what *he* knows, 'n' believe me he's got a directory beat to a custard. He hands us some info about everybody who's alive in Mount Clinton 'n' then starts in on the cemetery. He works back till he's talkin' about some 'dead an' gone these twenty year,' as he says.

"I happens to look at Peewee - Peewee's in a trance. He can't look away. He's noddin' his head 'n' his eyes has got a glassy stare. I goes outside quick 'n' lays up against the side of the buildin'.

"When I get back the old gazink is still workin' on Peewee, but all of a sudden he stops 'n' listens.

"'Pit-too-ee - there's your car, boys!' he says, 'n' then I begins to hear a groanin' sound.

"Man! they ain't no way to tell you about that street-car! She falls to pieces only they wraps all the upper parts together with wire till she looks like a birdcage. A big freckled guy with red hair is runnin' her 'n' I know just by lookin' at him it's Orphy.

"'Howdy, boys,' he says to us when he gets to where we're standin'. 'Jump aboard! I'm goin' down far as the pumpin' station an' the brakes ain't workin' just like they'd ought-a this mornin'.'

"'We've got a trunk,' I says.

"'Oh!' he says, 'n' spins the whirligig. She keeps right on goin'. Then he runs back 'n' yanks the trolley off, 'n' she begins to slow down. 'Git your trunk an' fetch it to where I stop at!' he hollers. 'The cut-off ain't workin' just like it ought-a this mornin'.'

"We lugs the trunk down to the car 'n' puts her on the back platform.

"'That's the way things goes!' says Orphy. 'I hadn't figgered on no trunk. Ed never tells me nothin' about it. You better set on it,' he says. 'The seats ain't just in first-class shape this mornin'.' I looks inside at the seats, 'n' he's got it doped right - some chickens has spent the night on 'em.

"After we gets to goin' Orphy pokes his head in the door.

"'The company don't allow me to handle the money,' he says. 'But my friends most gen'ally drop the fare down the right-hand side of the slot.'

"Me 'n' Peewee goes forward 'n' looks at the money box. The front of the car has warped till there's a big crack in the right-hand side of the box you can see the platform through. I drops

John Taintor Foote

two nickels in on that side, 'n' bing! they go down the shoot 'n' out the crack. They falls on the platform 'n' Orphy picks 'em up 'n' goes south with 'em.

"'That's what I call a live guy!' says Peewee. 'I'm proud to know him.'

"Pretty soon Orphy comes back 'n' jerks the trolley off 'n' we stop on a big square with a monument in the middle.

"'We got to wait here at the Public Square fer Mrs. Boone,' he says.

"In about twenty minutes here comes a dame across the Square. She's sixteen hands high 'n' will girt according. She belongs in the heavy-draft class 'n' she's puffin' some.

"'How-dee-do, Orphy,' she says. 'I'm a mite late, but I didn't get shet of my peach butter as quick as I aimed to.'

"'That's all right, Missus Boone,' says Orphy. 'The company allows me a liberal schedool. Set right down on the trunk, Missus Boone. I wouldn't resk the seats this mornin' if I was you.'

"'What's wrong with 'em?' says Mrs. Boone, 'n' pokes her head in the door. 'Land a Liberty!' she says. 'I shall certainly write to the *Banner* about this! I call it disgraceful!' Then she sets down on the trunk.

"I'm standin' up, but Peewee's still on it. She covers the whole trunk, but a little corner, 'n' Peewee tries to set on that.

"'Why don't you give the lady some room?' I says to Peewee, 'n' he gets up 'n' leaves her have the trunk.

"'You're a real polite young man,' says Mrs. Boone to me.

"We ain't more'n got started when the dame lets out a holler.

"'Orphy!' she yells, 'Stop! Wait a minute! Whoa!' Orphy comes 'n' yanks off the trolley.

"'I declare to goodness!' says Mrs. Boone. 'I've furgot my rubbers. Run up and get them for me, Orphy - they're behind the door in the front hall.'

"'I'd like to oblige you real well, Mrs. Boone,' says Orphy, 'but the company don't allow me to leave the car when I'm on duty -'

"'Well, I call lookin' after your customers bein' on duty,' says Mrs. Boone. 'Now, you skip an' get my rubbers, Orphy Shanner!'

"Orphy beats it fur the rubbers.

"While he's gone Mrs. Boone goes 'n' drops a nickel down the chute, but she don't put it in the right side 'n' it trickles down into the box. When Orphy gets the car started after he's back, he turns 'round 'n' gives a sad look at the nickel in the box.

"'Stung!' says Peewee, 'n' I think he's goin' to fall off the car.

"'What ails that young man?' says Mrs. Boone to me. 'He seems to be havin' a spell.'

"'It ain't nothin',' I says. 'He'll be all right in a minute.'

"We lets Mrs. Boone off after while 'n' keeps on goin' fur a mile or so till we come to some gates. In gold letters over the gates is 'Ohio's Beauty Spot,' 'n' below that in bigger letters yet is 'Lake Minnehaha Park.' We goes through these gates 'n' there's the track. More'n half the center-field is took up by a baseball diamond. In the other half is a pond with a shoot-the-chutes runnin' down into it.

"'Where's the lake?' Peewee says to Orphy.

"'Right in front of your nose,' says Orphy, pointin' at

the pond.

"'She's some body of water,' says Peewee. 'If you ain't careful a big rough guy'll come along here with a tin cup some dark night 'n' go south with her.'

"'I guess not,' says Orphy. 'She's four feet deep - in spots.'

"When we come in sight of the stalls, there's Butsy standin' in the rain with the hosses. A big bunch of Jaspers is holdin' a meetin' out in front of a row of bran'-new stalls that's just been put up. There's a hot argument goin' on 'n' they don't pay no attention to the rain.

"'You gone dippy?' I says to Butsy. 'What are you standin' out in the rain with the dogs fur? Why don't you put 'em up?'

"'No chance,' says Butsy. 'All the stalls is took except these new ones, 'n' the guy who furnished the lumber fur 'em won't unlock 'em till he's paid.'

"I looks at the stalls - there's a great big padlock on each door.

"'Why don't they slip him the coin?' I says.

"'You can search me,' says Butsy. 'That's what they're chewin' the rag about now.'

"Me 'n' Peewee slides over to where the crowd is.

"'I'll have the law on ye sure!' a old Jasper is sayin'. He's got on a long-tailed coat 'n' a white string tie.

"'Edge right in!' whispers Peewee to me. 'It ain't goin' to cost you a cent!'

"'You ain't got no right to lock them stalls, Jim Burns!' says the old Jasper. 'They belong to the Knox County Agricultural Society!'

"'Not till I'm paid fer the lumber, they don't!' says the guy he calls Jim Burns. 'Gimme eighty-six dollars, Kurnel, if you want to use them stalls.'

"'I'll have the law on ye sure as my name's Hunter!' says the old Jasper.

"'I guess you won't,' says Burns. 'My lawyer tells me to lock them stalls.'

"'Who's your lawyer?' says the old Jasper.

"Harry Evans," says Burns.

"'Well, why ain't he here?' says the old Jasper.

"'That's right - he'd ought to be here!' says several in the crowd.

"'I told him to come two hours ago,' says Burns. 'Say, Orphy! Telephone in an' find out why Harry ain't here!'

"Orphy climbs off the car 'n' goes in a shed 'n' we hears the telephone bell jingle. Pretty soon he comes back.

"'Missus Evans says Harry's fixin' a clock,' says Orphy. 'He's purty nigh through, an' he aims to git out here soon as she'll strike right. He's comin' in his autymobile.'

"The crowd gives a groan. Burns throws up his hands.

"'He'd a damn sight better walk,' he says.

"The argument sort-a dies down while they're waitin' fur this Harry Evans.

"'Come on!' Peewee says to me. 'I got to tell Butsy the good news.'

John Taintor Foote

"I see the rain tricklin' off Butsy's nose when we get close to him.

"'Stay with it, Butsy!' says Peewee. 'They got a lawyer comin' in a auto -'

"'Come 'n' hold these dogs fur a while!' says Butsy.

"'I'd like to,' says Peewee, 'but I can't. I might miss somethin',' 'n' he goes back to where the crowd is.

"We waits fur about a hour.

"'Why don't ye git a lawyer that ain't got no autymobile?' says somebody to Burns.

"'They've all got 'em,' says Burns. 'I'll give ye a dollar fer every lawyer in Mount Clinton ye can name who ain't got one of the blame things!'

"'How about Sam Koons?' says somebody.

"'Got one just the other day,' says Burns. 'It's made up to Bucyrus. It's called the Speeding Queen. He give three hundred and twenty dollars cash fer it.'

"Not long after that I begins to notice a noise. It ain't like any other sound I ever hears before. It gets right into my system. It's gettin' closer 'n' pretty soon I think I'll go find a nail 'n' bite on it.

"'What's that?' says Peewee.

"'It's him,' says Burns. 'It's Harry. If he don't have no bad luck he'll be here in twenty minutes. He ain't over a half a mile away right now.'

"'I hope they ain't no children on the road,' says Peewee.

"I figgers this Harry Evans is sure ridin' a threshin'-machine with its insides loose, but when he comes through the gates I gets a shock. Say, - his machine ain't much bigger'n a good-sized sardine can! It's painted red 'n' smoke's comin' out of the front of it. I can roll faster'n it's movin', but it keeps a-shakin' so he can't hardly set in the seat.

"When it's pretty close I see he's a little guy with specs 'n' a yellow coat on, but he's bein' shook so I can't hardly see what he does look like.

"'How-dee-do!' he says, when he gets her stopped. 'Er, - it occurs to me that I may be a little late. . . . Will any of you gentlemen indulge in a Cuban Beauty?' He fishes some long black stogies out of his pocket, but they don't nobody go against 'em, except him - he lights one.

"Then the crowd shows him the locked stalls 'n' everybody takes a shot at tellin' him what ought to be did.

"'Er, - it occurs to me,' says this Harry Evans, 'that there is a simple way out of the - er - difficulty.'

"'There's class to him,' says Peewee.

"'How's that?' says some one in the crowd.

"'If Colonel Hunter here will tender me - er - eighty-six dollars in behalf of my client,' says Harry Evans, 'I'll instruct my client to unlock the stalls.'

"'There you are!' says Peewee.

"The big Jasper lets out a fierce roar.

"'Not by a damn sight!' says he. 'We leased these grounds with the full use an' privilege of all buildin's an' other fixtures an' appurtenances fur the purpose of holdin' a fair. We weren't aimin' to get skinned out of eighty-six dollars by no lumber

John Taintor Foote

concern, 'n' we ain't a-goin' to neither!'

"'Let's see your lease?' says Harry Evans.

"'It's back in town at my office,' says the old Jasper.

"'Who signed it?' says Harry Evans.

"'Judge Tate signed it,' says the old Jasper.

"'Er, - if that's the case,' says Harry Evans, 'get him out here. He's receiver for the Park Company and you can make him pay this claim.'

"The whole bunch says that's a good idea. So they tell Orphy to go in 'n' get this Judge Tate.

"'I got to go 'n' tell Butsy there's a judge comin'!' says Peewee.

"'Butsy's sore about somethin',' he says when he gets back.

"This Judge Tate unloads hisself from the car when Orphy brings him, like he's the most important piece of work fur miles around. He has little side-whiskers 'n' a bay-window with a big gold chain stretched across it. He holds a umbrella over hisself with one hand 'n' wiggles the watch-chain with the other.

"'Ahem - gentlemen, what can I do for you?' he says.

"'Something doing now!' says Peewee to me. 'This is God-a'mighty's right-hand man!'

"'Er - Judge,' says Harry Evans, 'we are having a dispute concerning certain buildings on these premises, and - er - it occurred to me you could settle the matter.'

"'Settle is the word,' says Peewee to me.

"'As receiver for the Park Company, Judge,' says Harry Evans, 'can you tell us - er - who the buildings on these premises belong to?'

"'Why - ahem -' says the judge, 'it is my understanding that all the buildings of every sort and description belong to the Park Company, irrespective of any improvements that the - ahem - lessees may see fit to make.'

"'Now yer talkin',' says Burns. 'Just hand me eighty-six dollars due fer lumber on them new stalls - you claim to own em.

"'A-he-m!' says the judge. 'That's a different matter. The Agricultural Society is responsible for those stalls. The man you should see about your claim is Alf Dingle. I happen to know there is a certain sum of money in the treasury and I kind of think Alf will pay this claim. Why don't you try to get him to come out here?'

"They argue a while 'n' then it's thought best to send fur Alf Dingle. But Orphy has took the street-car 'n' went.

"'That's the way it goes,' says the old Jasper they call colonel. 'He's a-chasin' around town with that car instead of stayin' here tendin' to his business!'

"'I'll go in and get Alf,' says Harry Evans, startin' fur his machine.

"Nobody says nothin'.

"'I ain't got the heart to tell Butsy,' says Peewee.

"Harry Evans begins to turn the handle on his machine. He turns it fur ten minutes. When he's all in, he straightens up.

"'Somebody'll have to help me crank her,' he says.

John Taintor Foote

"The crowd goes to work. They all take turns. But she don't start.

"'Er - it occurs to me there may be something wrong with her,' says Harry Evans, 'n' starts to lift off the cover where the machinery is. Peewee gives me a poke in the ribs.

"'I expect he's right,' he says.

"'I'm gettin' all-fired tired of this putterin' around,' says the old Jasper. 'Tom', he says to a guy in overalls, 'get a crowbar an' knock them padlocks off.'

"'If you do that I'll put ye in jail!' yells Burns. 'That's a criminal act! It's destruction of property with burglarious intent! Ain't it, Harry?'

"Harry comes up out of the machinery. There's grease even on his specs.

"'It's the carbureter,' he says.

"'I'll leave it to the judge!' hollers Burns. 'Ain't that a criminal act?'

"'A - hem!' says the judge, 'I am not prepared to say you have the right to those stalls, but I wouldn't advise breaking a lock. As you say, it's a criminal act.'

"Just then here comes Orphy rollin' through the gates.

"'You hustle in an' git Alf Dingle!' says the old Jasper to him. 'An' when you git back, you stay here where you're needed!'

"The crowd has moved 'round back of the stalls to watch Harry Evans work on his machine. I stands with 'em fur a while, but Peewee has left. All of a sudden I see him poke his head 'round the end of the new stalls 'n' give me the high sign.

"'What you standin' out in the rain fur?' he says, when I gets near him.

"'What else can I do?' I says.

"'Come on 'n' I'll show you,' says Peewee.

"He leads me round in front of the stalls. In two of 'em is the hosses all bedded down nice. Butsy is settin' in the stall with his stud. He makes a puddle wherever he sets.

"'How did you get 'em open?' I says.

"'They ain't locked,' says Peewee. 'None of 'em are. The padlocks is closed, *but not locked*.'

"*No*,' I says.

"'It's the truth!' says Peewee, 'n' we rolls in the straw a-holdin' to each other till I feel like I'd been stepped on by a draft hoss.

"Butsy gets up.

"'Just one more snicker out of either of you,' he says, "n' I lead my hoss to the depot!'

"I see he means it 'n' I gets my head down in the straw 'n' holds my breath. Butsy stands there a-lookin' at us.

"'Has Alf come yet?' says Peewee, but he don't look at me.

"'Not yet, but he's expected,' I says, 'n' Peewee sticks his head down in the straw 'n' makes a noise like Harry Evans' machine. I does the same.

"As soon as I can see again, there's Butsy leadin' his hoss fur the gate.

"'Now you've done it,' I says to Peewee.

"Peewee sets up 'n' takes a look.

"'Hi, Butsy!' he yells, 'come on back here! We weren't laughin' at you!'

"But Butsy keeps right on a-goin'."

THE BIG TRAIN

The moon had acted as a stimulant to my thoughts, and the contented munching sound as the "string" of horses consumed their hay was not sedative enough to calm my utter wide-awake-ness.

"Why have you put bars across the door of that stall?" I asked Blister Jones, trying to rouse him from his placid mood. He pulled a straw from the bale upon which we sat, before replying.

"The Big Train's in there," he said quietly.

"No; is that a fact?" I cried, as I jumped to my feet and walked to the door across which were the heavy wooden bars that had attracted my attention. Peering through these I could see nothing, nor was there any sound toward which I might have strained my eyes.

"I guess he's not at home," I said. "I can't see him."

"Stick around that door 'n' you'll see him all right!" Blister assured me. Scarcely had he finished when the straw rustled and a huge head shot forward into the planes of moonlight that slanted between the bars into the black mystery of the stall.

Never had I seen anything so malevolent as this head. Its eyes were green flame, holding the hate of hell in their depths. The

John Taintor Foote

mouth was open, and the great white teeth closed with a snap on one of the bars and shook it in its socket.

So this was the noted man-killer, nicknamed because of his size and his astonishing ability to carry weight - The Big Train! His fame had been borne by leaded column beyond the racing, and to the more general public; for on several occasions he had succeeded in furnishing the yellow newspapers with gory copy.

He had begun his career as a man-killer in his three-year-old form. An unscrupulous owner had directed the jockey to carry an electric battery during an important race. Under the current The Big Train had run like a wild thing, and despite a staggering load placed on him by the handicapper, had won by many lengths.

After the race the stallion had reached back, and getting the jockey's leg between his teeth, had torn him from the saddle. Then before a screaming, horror-stricken grand-stand he had stamped the boy into a red waste.

This was his first and last public atrocity. He had killed men since, but always when they were alone with him. No one had seen him at his murders. He would have been destroyed when his racing days were over, but he possessed the ability to transmit a large measure of his stamina and speed to his offspring, and was greatly in demand as a sire.

I stood before The Big Train's stall, fascinated by his wicked attempts to get at me until Blister's attention was attracted by the thud of the stallion's hoofs against the lower door.

"Come on back here 'n' set down 'n' let that hoss get his rest,' he ordered. I obeyed.

"Why on earth did you take him?" I asked, when once more seated on the bale of straw.

"Well, ole Prindle says he'd give fifty bucks a week to the guy who'll handle him 'n' I needs the money . . . fur certain reasons."

"Fur certain reasons" was added diffidently, I thought. This was an altogether new quality in Blister. And I remembered the pretty, spoiled-looking, young girl I had seen with him quite often of late. She was rosy, pouty, slim, enticing and thoroughly aware of how desirable she appeared. Blister had told me she was his landlady's daughter, and I knew she lived but a block from the race track. I thought of the head I had seen, and felt certain that fifty *thousand* a week would not tempt me into an intimate relationship with its owner.

"I can't tell you how sorry I am you've taken him - it's a fearful risk," I said.

"Get out!" said Blister. "He won't even muss my hair. I never go in to him alone 'n' he don't like company fur his little stunts. He's a regular family hoss in a crowd."

Two stable-boys now climbed the track fence and came toward us rather hastily.

"Been on a vacation?" was Blister's greeting to them.

"Playin' seven-up 'n' tried to finish the game," one of them explained as they started with buckets for the pump.

"That's good. It don't matter whether these hosses get watered, just so you swipes enjoy yourselves," Blister commented.

I watched languidly while the buckets were filled and brought to the horses, until this process reached the barred stall. Then I became interested. One of the boys approached the stall with a bucket in one hand and a pitchfork held near the pronged end in the other. He swung open the lower door and whacked the fork handle back and forth inside, yelling harsh commands in the meantime. He succeeded in getting the bucket where the horse could drink, but the pitchfork was seized and twisted

John Taintor Foote

and the boy had difficulty in wrenching it away. It was all he could do to regain possession of it.

"Little pink toes is feelin' like his ole sweet self again," said Blister. "I been worried about him - he's seemed so pie-faced here lately."

"Don't worry none about him," said the boy who had watered The Big Train. "Mama's lamb ain't forgot his cute ways." Then he addressed the other boy. "Say, Chic, you snored somethin' fierce last night! Why don't you sleep in here with Bright Eyes, so's not to disturb me?"

"Would, only I might thrash around in my sleep 'n' hurt him," promptly replied the other boy.

Two figures had come from the street, through the gate and strolled down the line of stalls. One of them was feminine, and in white, and as they drew nearer, "Good evening, Mister Jones," floated to us in an assured though girlish voice.

It was the landlady's daughter, attended by a cavalier in the person of a stolid young man of German extraction, as I thought at first glance, and this was confirmed by Blister's, "Let me make you acquainted with Miss Malloy," and "Shake hands with Mister Shultz."

Then began the by no means unskilful playing of one lover against the other. She sat, a queen - the bale of straw a throne - and dispensed royal favors impartially; a dimple melting to a smile, a frown changed by feminine magic into a delicious pout.

In the moonlight she was exceedingly lovely. She seemed unapproachable, elusive, mysterious, and yet her art touched the material. She contrived to bring out how successful Mister Shultz was in the bakery business, and in the next breath told nonchalantly of the vast sums acquired by a race-horse trainer.

She appealed to Blister to corroborate this.

"Isn't that so, Mister Jones? Didn't you tell me you get fifty dollars a week for training one horse?"

Blister was not above impressing his rival, it seemed. He nodded to this deceptive question. And since he had nine horses in his "string," the worthy German's eyes bulged.

At last I rose to go and our little circle broke up. The girl, with a coquettish good night to me, moved away from us and stood with her back to the stalls, her face lifted to the moon.

"Good night, ole Four Eyes!" said Blister, and gave my hand a friendly pressure, just as a rattling sound attracted my eyes to the barred stall.

The lower door was swinging open. A powerful neck had tossed the bars from their sockets. This was the rattle I had heard, as Death came out of that stall, huge and terrible, to rear above the unconscious white figure in the moonlight.

My look of horror swung Blister about. I saw him dive headlong, and the white figure was knocked to safety as the man-killer's forefeet struck Blister down.

The rest was a dream . . . I found myself beating with futile fists the giant body that rose and fell as it stamped upon that other body beneath. I knew, but dimly, that the night was pierced by shriek on shriek. And still I felt the rise and fall of the beast. How long it lasted I do not know. . . . . . .

A helmeted figure swept me aside, I saw a gleam in the moonlight - a flash, and felt that a shot was fired, although I can not remember hearing it. The Big Train ceased to rise and fall. He swayed, staggered and crumpled to the ground.

"An ambulance - quick!" I said to the heaven-sent policeman; and saw him start for the gate on a lumbering trot. Then I stooped to the figure, lying with its head in what the moonlight had changed to a pool of ink.

Suddenly I felt a woman's soft form beneath my hands. It was in white and it covered that other dreadful figure with its own . . . and moaned.

"This won't do," I said to the girl. "Let me see how badly he's hurt."

She took Blister's head in her arms.

"Go 'way from here! He's dead," she said. "He saved me . . . he's mine! Go 'way from here!"

A crowd was forming. I sent a stableboy for a blanket, put it under Blister's head, despite the girl's protests, and pulled her roughly to her feet.

"Go over to that bale and sit down!" I ordered, giving her a shake; and to my surprise she obeyed. "Sit with her!" I said to the German, and I heard her repeat, "Go 'way from here!" as he approached. . . .

The ambulance clanged through the gate. The young surgeon put his ear to Blister's heart, picked the limp body up unaided and placed it in the somber-looking vehicle.

"Beat it, Max!" he said to the driver.

"What hospital?" I called after him.

"Saint Luke's!" he shouted, as they gathered speed.

"You had better take her home now," I suggested to Mr. Shultz. "I am going to the hospital."

"So am I," said the girl. "Tell mother," she directed at the German, as she started for the gate.

"You'd better not go," I remonstrated. "I'll let you know everything as soon as I hear."

She paid not the slightest attention. When we reached the street she stopped on the wrong corner waiting for a car that would have taken her away from, instead of toward, the hospital.

"You can't go down-town like this!" I said, making a last effort. "Look at your dress!" and I pointed to the front of her gown - a bright crimson under the electric light.

She looked down at herself and shuddered.

"I'll go if it's the last thing I do," she said. "You can save your breath."

The car was all but empty. The girl sat staring, dry-eyed, straight before her. A dirty old woman, seeing the set face and blood-stained dress, leaned eagerly across the aisle.

"Has the young lady been hurt?" she wheezed.

"None of your business," said Miss Malloy. And the old woman subsided at this shaft of plain truth.

Our ride was half completed when my companion began to speak, in a broken monotone. She addressed no one in particular. If was as though conscience spoke through unconscious lips.

"And I've been foolin' with him just like all the rest - I thought it was smart! I never knew, for sure, till back there, and now *he'll* never know . . . he'll not hear me when I tell it to him." Suddenly the monotone grew shrill. "*He'll never hear nothing of what Eve found out!*"

"Quiet! Quiet!" I said, and took her hand. "He's only hurt. The doctors will bring him around all right."

"No," she said. "I've been foolin' with him. I've been wicked and mean, and it's been sent to punish me."

A house surgeon and the engulfing odor of iodoform met us at the door of the emergency ward, whither we were led by a nurse.

"We can't tell anything before tomorrow," answered the surgeon to my question. "The pulse is fairly strong, and that means hope."

"I must see him," the girl stated.

"Sorry," said the surgeon, shaking his head. "No visitors allowed in this ward at night."

Two eyes, big and dark and beseeching, were raised to his. They shone from the white face and plead with him.

"Oh, doctor . . . *please!*" was all she said, but the eyes won her battle.

The nurse joined forces with the eyes. She looked past the surgeon.

"Very few in here to-night, Doctor Brandt," she urged.

"I wonder what would become of hospital rules if we left it to you nurses!" he protested, as he stepped aside and gently drew the girl within.

Down the dim aisle between the snowy beds we went, until the surgeon stopped at one, beside which sat a nurse, her fingers on the wrist of the bandaged occupant.

One bloodless hand picked feebly at the covering. The girl took this in both her own and pressed it to her cheek. Then stooping even lower, she cooed to the head on the pillow.

"The Big Train's pulled in . . ." muttered a far voice from between the bandages.

"Railroad man - isn't he?" inquired the surgeon of me.

"No. A horseman," I replied.

"He talks about trains. Was it a railroad accident?"

"He was injured by a horse called The Big Train," I explained.

"Oh - that one," he said, enlightened.

"Why don't they shoot him?"

"They did," I said.

"Good!" exclaimed the surgeon. "That is fine!"

After taking the girl to her home, I sent telegrams to "Mr. Van," as I had heard Blister call him - one to Morrisville, New Jersey, and one to the Union Club, New York. Judge and Mrs. Dillon were abroad.

When I had telephoned to the hospital the next morning, I went to the office and found a message on my desk. It read:

"Have everything possible done. Send all bills to me. He must come here to convalesce."

It was headed Morrisville, and was signed, "W. D. Van Voast."

That same day Blister was taken to a big, airy, private room with two nurses in attendance.

For a time it seemed hopeless. And then the fates decided to spare that valiant whimsical spirit and Death drew slowly back. The stallion had been unshod, and to this and the semi-darkness Blister owed his life.

I had met the girl frequently at the hospital and at last they told us we could see Blister for a moment the next day. Ten o'clock was the time set and as we sat in the visitor's room together, waiting, she seemed worried.

"You should be more cheerful," I said. "The danger is past, or we would not be allowed to see him."

"It isn't that," she replied. "I used to like horses. Now every horse I see scares me to death." Then she hesitated and looked at me timidly.

"Well," I encouraged, "that's natural, what of it?"

"I've been thinking -" she said slowly, "every girl should like what her husb -" she stopped and blushed till she looked like a rose in confusion.

"Oh, I see what you mean," I said in a matter-of-fact tone. "Since you care for Blister, you feel that you should also be interested in his profession."

"That's it! You say things just right!" she exclaimed gratefully.

"You will get over this dread of horses," I assured her. "Because there are murderers in the world you do not fear all men. Occasionally there are bad horses, just as there are bad people. You shouldn't judge all the splendid faithful creatures who spend their lives serving us, by one vicious brute."

"Oh, I know that!" she said. "And I'll try as hard as ever I can to get over it."

"This is quite a little woman . . . she has developed," I thought.

An unknown Blister with strange cavernous eyes, lay in the room to which we were presently taken. I stood at the foot of the bed, directly in his line of vision, but he did not seem to recognize me. He looked through and beyond me. At last -

"Hello, Four Eyes!" came feebly from him. Slowly he became conscious of the girl's face, looking down into his own. "You here, too?" he questioned.

"Yes, dear," she said tremblingly.

The sight of the poor sick face was too much for her and she knelt hastily to hide the tears. Then the round curve of her young bosom was indented by his wasted shoulder as she bent and kissed him on the mouth.

A woeful scar across his cheek reddened against the white skin. A flash of the old Blister appeared in the hollow eyes.

"There's class to that!" he said.

John Taintor Foote

Choose from Thousands of 1stWorldLibrary Classics By

A. M. Barnard
Ada Leverson
Adolphus William Ward
Aesop
Agatha Christie
Alexander Aaronsohn
Alexander Kielland
Alexandre Dumas
Alfred Gatty
Alfred Ollivant
Alice Duer Miller
Alice Turner Curtis
Alice Dunbar
Allen Chapman
Ambrose Bierce
Amelia E. Barr
Amory H. Bradford
Andrew Lang
Andrew McFarland Davis
Andy Adams
Anna Alice Chapin
Anna Sewell
Annie Besant
Annie Hamilton Donnell
Annie Payson Call
Annie Roe Carr
Annonaymous
Anton Chekhov
Arnold Bennett
Arthur Conan Doyle
Arthur M. Winfield
Arthur Ransome
Arthur Schnitzler
Atticus
B.H. Baden-Powell
B. M. Bower
B. C. Chatterjee
Baroness Emmuska Orczy
Baroness Orczy
Basil King
Bayard Taylor
Ben Macomber
Bertha Muzzy Bower
Bjornstjerne Bjornson
Booth Tarkington
Boyd Cable
Bram Stoker
C. Collodi
C. E. Orr

C. M. Ingleby
Carolyn Wells
Catherine Parr Traill
Charles A. Eastman
Charles Amory Beach
Charles Dickens
Charles Dudley Warner
Charles Farrar Browne
Charles Ives
Charles Kingsley
Charles Klein
Charles Hanson Towne
Charles Lathrop Pack
Charles Romyn Dake
Charles Whibley
Charles Willing Beale
Charlotte M. Braeme
Charlotte M. Yonge
Charlotte Perkins Stetson
Clair W. Hayes
Clarence Day Jr.
Clarence E. Mulford
Clemence Housman
Confucius
Coningsby Dawson
Cornelis DeWitt Wilcox
Cyril Burleigh
D. H. Lawrence
Daniel Defoe
David Garnett
Dinah Craik
Don Carlos Janes
Donald Keyhoe
Dorothy Kilner
Dougan Clark
Douglas Fairbanks
E. Nesbit
E.P.Roe
E. Phillips Oppenheim
Earl Barnes
Edgar Rice Burroughs
Edith Van Dyne
Edith Wharton
Edward Everett Hale
Edward J. O'Biren
Edward S. Ellis
Edwin L. Arnold
Eleanor Atkins
Eliot Gregory

Elizabeth Gaskell
Elizabeth McCracken
Elizabeth Von Arnim
Ellem Key
Emerson Hough
Emilie F. Carlen
Emily Dickinson
Enid Bagnold
Enilor Macartney Lane
Erasmus W. Jones
Ernie Howard Pie
Ethel May Dell
Ethel Turner
Ethel Watts Mumford
Eugenie Foa
Eugene Wood
Eustace Hale Ball
Evelyn Everett-green
Everard Cotes
F. H. Cheley
F. J. Cross
F. Marion Crawford
Federick Austin Ogg
Ferdinand Ossendowski
Francis Bacon
Francis Darwin
Frances Hodgson Burnett
Frances Parkinson Keyes
Frank Gee Patchin
Frank Harris
Frank Jewett Mather
Frank L. Packard
Frank V. Webster
Frederic Stewart Isham
Frederick Trevor Hill
Frederick Winslow Taylor
Friedrich Kerst
Friedrich Nietzsche
Fyodor Dostoyevsky
G.A. Henty
G.K. Chesterton
Gabrielle E. Jackson
Garrett P. Serviss
Gaston Leroux
George A. Warren
George Ade
Geroge Bernard Shaw
George Durston
George Ebers

George Eliot
George Gissing
George MacDonald
George Meredith
George Orwell
George Sylvester Viereck
George Tucker
George W. Cable
George Wharton James
Gertrude Atherton
Gordon Casserly
Grace E. King
Grace Gallatin
Grace Greenwood
Grant Allen
Guillermo A. Sherwell
Gulielma Zollinger
Gustav Flaubert
H. A. Cody
H. B. Irving
H.C. Bailey
H. G. Wells
H. H. Munro
H. Irving Hancock
H. Rider Haggard
H. W. C. Davis
Haldeman Julius
Hall Caine
Hamilton Wright Mabie
Hans Christian Andersen
Harold Avery
Harold McGrath
Harriet Beecher Stowe
Harry Castlemon
Harry Coghill
Harry Houidini
Hayden Carruth
Helent Hunt Jackson
Helen Nicolay
Hendrik Conscience
Hendy David Thoreau
Henri Barbusse
Henrik Ibsen
Henry Adams
Henry Ford
Henry Frost
Henry James
Henry Jones Ford
Henry Seton Merriman
Henry W Longfellow
Herbert A. Giles

Herbert Carter
Herbert N. Casson
Herman Hesse
Hildegard G. Frey
Homer
Honore De Balzac
Horace B. Day
Horace Walpole
Horatio Alger Jr.
Howard Pyle
Howard R. Garis
Hugh Lofting
Hugh Walpole
Humphry Ward
Ian Maclaren
Inez Haynes Gillmore
Irving Bacheller
Isabel Hornibrook
Israel Abrahams
Ivan Turgenev
J.G.Austin
J. Henri Fabre
J. M. Barrie
J. Macdonald Oxley
J. S. Fletcher
J. S. Knowles
J. Storer Clouston
Jack London
Jacob Abbott
James Allen
James Andrews
James Baldwin
James Branch Cabell
James DeMille
James Joyce
James Lane Allen
James Lane Allen
James Oliver Curwood
James Oppenheim
James Otis
James R. Driscoll
Jane Austen
Jane L. Stewart
Janet Aldridge
Jens Peter Jacobsen
Jerome K. Jerome
John Burroughs
John Cournos
John F. Kennedy
John Gay
John Glasworthy

John Habberton
John Joy Bell
John Kendrick Bangs
John Milton
John Philip Sousa
Jonas Lauritz Idemil Lie
Jonathan Swift
Joseph A. Altsheler
Joseph Carey
Joseph Conrad
Joseph E. Badger Jr
Joseph Hergesheimer
Joseph Jacobs
Jules Vernes
Julian Hawthrone
Julie A Lippmann
Justin Huntly McCarthy
Kakuzo Okakura
Kenneth Grahame
Kenneth McGaffey
Kate Langley Bosher
Kate Langley Bosher
Katherine Cecil Thurston
Katherine Stokes
L. A. Abbot
L. T. Meade
L. Frank Baum
Latta Griswold
Laura Dent Crane
Laura Lee Hope
Laurence Housman
Lawrence Beasley
Leo Tolstoy
Leonid Andreyev
Lewis Carroll
Lewis Sperry Chafer
Lilian Bell
Lloyd Osbourne
Louis Hughes
Louis Tracy
Louisa May Alcott
Lucy Fitch Perkins
Lucy Maud Montgomery
Luther Benson
Lydia Miller Middleton
Lyndon Orr
M. Corvus
M. H. Adams
Margaret E. Sangster
Margret Howth
Margaret Vandercook

Margret Penrose
Maria Edgeworth
Maria Thompson Daviess
Mariano Azuela
Marion Polk Angellotti
Mark Overton
Mark Twain
Mary Austin
Mary Catherine Crowley
Mary Cole
Mary Hastings Bradley
Mary Roberts Rinehart
Mary Rowlandson
M. Wollstonecraft Shelley
Maud Lindsay
Max Beerbohm
Myra Kelly
Nathaniel Hawthrone
Nicolo Machiavelli
O. F. Walton
Oscar Wilde
Owen Johnson
P.G. Wodehouse
Paul and Mabel Thorne
Paul G. Tomlinson
Paul Severing
Percy Brebner
Peter B. Kyne
Plato
R. Derby Holmes
R. L. Stevenson
R. S. Ball
Rabindranath Tagore
Rahul Alvares
Ralph Bonehill
Ralph Henry Barbour
Ralph Victor
Ralph Waldo Emmerson
Rene Descartes
Rex Beach

Rex E. Beach
Richard Harding Davis
Richard Jefferies
Richard Le Gallienne
Robert Barr
Robert Frost
Robert Gordon Anderson
Robert L. Drake
Robert Lansing
Robert Lynd
Robert Michael Ballantyne
Robert W. Chambers
Rosa Nouchette Carey
Rudyard Kipling
Samuel B. Allison
Samuel Hopkins Adams
Sarah Bernhardt
Sarah C. Hallowell
Selma Lagerlof
Sherwood Anderson
Sigmund Freud
Standish O'Grady
Stanley Weyman
Stella Benson
Stella M. Francis
Stephen Crane
Stewart Edward White
Stijn Streuvels
Swami Abhedananda
Swami Parmananda
T. S. Ackland
T. S. Arthur
The Princess Der Ling
Thomas A. Janvier
Thomas A Kempis
Thomas Anderton
Thomas Bailey Aldrich
Thomas Bulfinch
Thomas De Quincey
Thomas Dixon

Thomas H. Huxley
Thomas Hardy
Thomas More
Thornton W. Burgess
U. S. Grant
Valentine Williams
Various Authors
Vaughan Kester
Victor Appleton
Victoria Cross
Virginia Woolf
Wadsworth Camp
Walter Camp
Walter Scott
Washington Irving
Wilbur Lawton
Wilkie Collins
Willa Cather
Willard F. Baker
William Dean Howells
William le Queux
W. Makepeace Thackeray
William W. Walter
William Shakespeare
Winston Churchill
Yei Theodora Ozaki
Yogi Ramacharaka
Young E. Allison
Zane Grey

www.ingramcontent.com/pod-product-compliance
Lightning Source LLC
Chambersburg PA
CBHW020502100426
42813CB00030B/3080/J